This book is to be returned on or before
the last date stamped below

PLYMOUTH POLYTECHNIC
LEARNING RESOURCES CENTRE
Telephone: (0752) 21312 ext.5413
(After 5p.m. (0752) 264661 weekdays only)

This book is subject to recall if required by another reader.
Books may be renewed by phone, please quote Telepen number.
CHARGES WILL BE MADE FOR OVERDUE BOOKS

Commercial Banks and
the Creditworthiness of
Less Developed Countries

Research for Business Decisions, No. 11

Other Titles in This Series

Commercial Banks and the Creditworthiness of Less Developed Countries

by
Yoon-Dae Euh

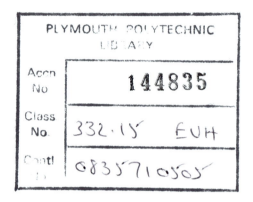
Produced and distributed by
University Microfilms International
Ann Arbor, Michigan 48106

Library of Congress Cataloging in Publication Data

Euh, Yoon-Dae, 1945-
    Commercial banks and the creditworthiness of
less developed countries.

    (Research for business decisions ; no. 11)
    Bibliography: p.
    Includes index.
    1. Underdeveloped areas—Loans, Foreign—Mathematical
models. 2. Underdeveloped areas—Debts, External—
Mathematical models. 3. Banks and banking.   I. Title.
II. Series.
HJ8899.F84   332.1'5   79-22721
ISBN 0-8357-1050-5

CONTENTS

Bank for International Settlement
Development Assistance Committee (Expanded
Reporting System)
Capital Market System
Debtor Reporting System

Creditworthiness Index (Dependent Variable)
Determinants of Creditworthiness
Estimation without political stability variable
Estimation with political stability variable
Stability of Model
Relationships with Other Models Using
Different creditworthiness indices

Limitations and Contributions of the Study

vi

TABLES

TABLE

FIGURES

CHAPTER I

INTRODUCTION: THE SIGNIFICANCE AND
PURPOSE OF PROPOSED STUDY

During the last few years, lending to the less developed countries (LDCs) has been one of the most serious issues facing the international capital markets because of the rapid increase in the volume of international capital flows to LDCs and the shift in the transfer mechanism from official sources to private commercial banks. The problem of financing LDCs is not new, but the focus of attention has shifted from LDCs' need for foreign credit and access to the international credit to one of the LDCs' ability to fulfill the obligations of existing and future external debts.

Until about 1970, LDCs with limited developmental capital or balance of payments deficits had to rely largely on foreign grants, IMF stand-by credit, suppliers credits, and development loans from official lending agencies of foreign governments as well as international financial institutions (see Table 1-1). Supplier and trade credit for financing exports from industrial countries was LDCs' major source of private loans until 1970, but much of that money was provided under the umbrella of foreign nations' official credit or insurance agencies.[1] This was supplemented by some direct bond placements in foreign capital markets. Borrowings of LDCs from foreign bond markets increased from $612 million for the decade 1956-65, to $380 million in 1970 alone. This funding was quite limited, however, compared to supplier credits of $2,297 million and relative to need for $11.1 billion represented by current account deficits in the same year.

During the 1970s the LDCs' access to commercial banks as well as international bond markets has increased steadily as shown in Table 1-2. Especially the worldwide recession and quadrupled oil prices of 1973-74 pushed LDCs' foreign exchange requirements (deficits on current account of balance of payments) far in excess of what they were likely to obtain from their traditional foreign official sources, despite the creation of a significant new official source of financing in the form of the IMF oil facility in 1974-75. While funds from foreign official sources to LDCs have increased consistently in absolute terms, they have been decreasing as a proportion of the total foreign exchange needs of LDCs. Thus LDCs must increasingly rely on commercial banks to meet the remaining financial needs.

Table 1-1

Total Flow of Funds (Disbursements) to LDCs (in U.S. $ million)

	1969	1970	1971	1972	1973	1974	1975
Total official	4838	5503	6040	6714	8845	10303	14611
Government	3711	4185	4421	4816	6333	6983	10199
International organizations	1127	1318	1619	1898	2512	3320	4412
Total private	4062	4733	5168	7409	10510	13357	17894
Suppliers	2083	2297	1919	2384	2415	3097	3670
Financial markets*	1955	2135	3243	5018	8091	10259	14197
Other private +	24	301	6	6	4	1	27
Total	8900	10236	11208	14123	19355	23660	32505

Note: Computations based on the public and publicly-guaranteed external debt disbursement of 84 countries.

*Loans from private banks and other private financial institutions plus publicly-issued and privately-placed bonds.

+ Debts resulting from nationalized properties, and unclassified debts.

Source: World Bank, *World Debt Tables*, EC-167/77.

According to World Bank statistics on the external debts of 84 developing countries[2] (shown in Table 1-3), official sources accounted for $31.7 billion or 62.9 percent of total disbursed outstanding debt, compared with $18.7 billion from private sources in 1969. By 1975 this amount had changed to $71.3 billion or 49.7 percent, from official sources and $72.4 billion from private sources.

Table 1–2

**Debt Outstanding (Disbursed) from Private Sources
(in U.S. $ billion)**

Year	Suppliers	Financial Markets		Other	Total
1969	6.7	5.8		0.7	13.3
1970	7.6	7.2	(28%)*	1.1	15.9
1971	8.4	9.3	(29%)	1.1	18.9
1972	9.2	12.6	(35%)	1.0	22.9
1973	10.0	18.3	(45%)	0.8	29.2
1974	11.4	25.6	(39%)	1.2	38.2
1975	12.1	36.5	(42%)	1.1	49.7

Note: Computations based on the public and publicly guaranteed external debt outstanding of 84 LDCs.

*( ): Annual growth rate.

Source: World Bank, *World Debt Tables*, EC-167/77.

Table 1–3

**Debt (Disbursed) from Official and Private Sources of LDCs
(in U.S. $ billion)**

	Official Sources	Private Sources		Total Private	Percentage of Private Sources in Total Debt
		Official Guaranteed	Other* Private		
1969	31.7	13.3	5.4	18.7	37.1
1970	35.3	15.9	6.4	22.3	38.7
1971	41.0	18.9	8.3	27.2	39.9
1972	46.0	22.9	12.5	35.4	43.5
1973	53.5	29.2	16.2	45.4	45.9
1974	61.9	38.2	20.1	58.3	48.5
1975	71.3	49.7	22.7	72.4	50.3

*Estimations of World Bank. The private debts which are neither public nor publicly guaranteed.

Source: World Bank, *World Debt Tables*, EC-167/77 and *The External Debt of Developing Countries (Memorandum)*, 1977.

Euromarket Borrowings

The rapid growth of the Euromarkets in the last few years has provided LDCs with large and easily accessible sources of capital. From less than $1.5 billion in 1971, the total amount of LDC bank loans from the Euromarkets increased to over $17 billion in 1976. The Euromarkets have certain operating advantages over the competing credit markets, the national markets for foreign borrowers -- the absence of reserve requirements and no limitations on interest ceilings or quantitative credit restrictions, the advantage of low tax location, and the efficiency achieved in handling large volumes of credit enable Euromarkets to operate on small margins, which accounts for their rapid growth. This, in turn, has given LDCs the opportunity to borrow on relatively favorable terms.

Most of the borrowing from the Euromarkets has been via medium-term syndicated credits[3] with floating interest rates. The syndicate involves a large number of banks, often 20 or more, so that the average individual share per bank is relatively small. Since no one international bank is willing to provide the full amount of a large loan, this technique enables banks to pool their funds and to distribute risks. "The actuarial spread of risks has enabled banks to lend to borrowers they might otherwise have shunned, and the major beneficiaries of this syndicate mechanic have been LDCs."[4]

Contrary to the favorable development in the private capital market, the advantages of borrowing from the official lending institutions have diminished. As the funds from their member governments become limited, the World Bank and regional development banks have had to act more and more as financial intermediaries, lending funds to LDCs which were borrowed from the private capital markets. As a result, the terms and conditions at which they lend to LDCs approach more and more those stipulated by the private lenders. While the official lenders are still likely to offer longer maturity periods, and lower interest rates, the interest rate advantage has diminished for many creditworthy LDCs which now can borrow directly from the Euromarkets at relatively small premiums above the prevailing minimum lending rate.

Some countries prefer to borrow from commercial banks rather than meet the stricter conditions on monetary policies and economic performances that the lending agencies, especially IMF, mandate. For example, Euromarkets loans are advantageous in that

1. They can be obtained relatively quickly, with a minimum of red tape;
2. There are no requirements that the projects they finance be carried out on the basis of international competitive bidding;

3. The goods and services financed are not tied to any stipulated country of origin;
4. The loan need not be tied to a project nor need it cover only imports. It may be a simple balance-of-payments loan, or it may be used to restructure a country's external or even internal debt;
5. The credits may enable the borrower to switch indebtedness from currencies that are appreciating relative to its own to currencies that are expected to maintain their parity or even depreciate (if the borrower could anticipate the change in exchange rates correctly);
6. They enable the borrower to take advantage of possible declines in the cost of money, since the interest rate is variable.[5]

But borrowing from the Euromarkets also involves some risks, as a result of its commercial character and also of its technical features.[6] First, the bases for the interest rate, the three-month and six-month Eurorates, have been highly volatile depending on changing market conditions and uncertainties in the international capital market. These volatile rates not only increase the uncertainty to borrowers on the future interest rates, but also make it difficult for borrowers to evaluate the cost of the loan over its life. Second, since the average maturity of Eurocredits, from five to seven years, is shorter than that offered by official sources, the maturity may not be long enough for the developmental project financed by the Eurocredits to generate sufficient cash flow to amortize its cost. Third, there is no assurance of the continuity of Eurocurrency flows to LDCs. Should traditional borrowers in developed countries increase their demand for Eurocurrencies, the result might be not only higher interest rates but also a reallocation of credits favoring them at the expense of LDCs. These risks and uncertainty features are accepted as inevitable by LDCs who seek to achieve their economic goals without the delay of relying on foreign capital.

Assessing Creditworthiness

The shift in the transfer mechanism of the international capital flow from official sources to private commercial banks, in combination with ever-increasing borrowings of LDCs, has given rise to concerns about "the optimum amount of foreign borrowings," and "How to assess the creditworthiness of LDCs." Unlike the foreign official sources and international financial institutions providing "soft" loans, commercial banks as profit-maximizing entities are concerned more with the risks of lending. In addition, the widespread reports about the economic problems and consequent debt rescheduling of several LDCs which had been major Euromarket borrowers, has intensified the need to establish an appropriate framework for risk analysis.

Each bank has its own criteria for assessing risk and the debt repayment capability of a country. But evaluation of credit and risk is normally conducted by the bank that leads the syndicate when the lending to an LDC is a syndicated credit. The participating banks are assumed to be responsible for their own judgments, based on the information provided by the lead bank, in deciding to participate in a syndicated credit. To prevent the possible disclaimers, the lead bank treats the preparation of placement memoranda as if they were prospectuses, obtaining "warranties from borrowers as to the accuracy of information and representation."[7] It also takes more care in disseminating information concerning the credit both at the time of its arrangement and throughout its duration. Therefore the ultimate responsibility for evaluating a borrower's creditworthiness lies on the shoulders of the lead bank, and this will impel the lead bank to develop a more reliable system of data gathering and evaluation of information.

At present most of the evaluations are based on the qualitative analysis of an index system which uses a number of common indicators, such as debt service ratio and the level of reserves to imports. There are few publicized attempts to devise a reliable statistical method of identifying creditworthiness by either practitioners or scholars.

The purpose of this study is to identify the determinants of a country's creditworthiness. It presents a normative conceptual framework for creditworthiness within which relevant data and forecast can be conveniently analyzed, and attempts to empirically validate that framework.

To enhance understanding about the causes of creditworthiness, it evaluates the distinctive features of those countries which have had access to the private capital markets. The ability of a country to borrow from private capital markets at reasonable terms has been the most important criterion for judging creditworthiness used by international financial institutions such as IBRD, whether or not continued lending to a country is justified.[8]

One reason for lack of a reliable statistical study is that some key elements in assessing creditworthiness, i.e., political stability, willingness to repay, general economic management, and external debt management, can be hardly quantified to fit into the statistical model. Thus instead of utilizing statistical methods, bankers rely on first-hand experience and qualitative analysis to develop the composite index techniques of credit rating which do not require the exact quantification of the variables under consideration.

A more important reason for insufficient statistical study is that no single creditor has experienced any *outright* default of repayment by the country borrowing since the 1930s. There have been more than 33 multilateral debt rescheduling cases since 1956, which have provided about $8.7 billion in debt relief, excluding a number of bilateral reschedulings among individual creditors and debtors and a small multilateral rescheduling for Cambodia (see Table 1-4). But there has not been a single write-off on creditors' books for economic (balance of payments) reasons. In part this had occurred because governments of LDCs "have been less inclined to renege on commercial debt repayments than they sometimes are to nationalize foreign investments or to stop the repatriation of dividends and private capital, after political coups or in times of economic duress."[9]

The lack of defaulting makes it impossible to develop a model based on objective historical data. The dependent variable (creditworthiness) in the statistical model cannot be obtained even on an *ex post* basis. Empirical tests based on actual reschedulings solve the problem of objectivity. They provide information on reschedulings resulting from short-term liquidity difficulties, and thus indirectly on the possibility of outright default. But they do not answer the question on the outright default or creditworthiness of countries. The approach based on rescheduling does not necessarily measure the creditworthiness of a country, because it deals only with the liquidity problem of the country. Such short-term difficulties indicate a cash-flow problem, but do not necessarily indicate the country's inability to create additional output which is sufficient to cover the cost for input and debt service.

Dependent Variable for Creditworthiness

In this study the loan amounts from the private capital markets, adjusted for differences in external financing demand between countries, will be the dependent variable for creditworthiness. The loan amounts will be divided by the needs for external financing of a country, i.e., loan amount divided by needs, so that the dependent variable will become ultimately the creditworthiness index of a country and will have a value ranging between one and zero. (The rationale and mechanics of developing the needs for external financing of a country will be mentioned in Chapter III.) The reason for using the loan amount is that commercial banks lending to LDCs are more likely to differentiate country exposure limits.[10] Brackenridge asserts that "one of the principal reasons for an international bank to evaluate the creditworthiness is to establish exposure limits for individual countries, because the bank wants to distribute the present and potential risk assets of the bank on a country-by-country basis."[11]

THE CREDITWORTHINESS OF LDCs

Table 1–4

Multilateral Debt Reschedulings (1956-1976)

Country	Year	Amount Rescheduled (U.S. $ million)	Country	Year	Amount Rescheduled (U.S. $ million)
Argentina	1956	500		1973	187
	1962	240		1974	194
	1965	76		1975	167
				1976	160
Brazil	1961	300			
	1964	200	Indonesia	1966	247
				1967	85
Chile	1965	96		1968	85
	1972	160		1970	2,100
	1974	367			
	1975	230	Pakistan	1972	234
				1973	103
Ghana	1966	170		1974	650
	1968	100			
	1970	25	Peru	1968	58
	1974	290		1969	70
India	1968	300	Turkey	1959	400
	1971	92		1965	220
	1972	153		1972	114
			Zaire	1976	350
			Total		8,723

Note: Debt reschedulings in the table represent multilateral consolidations of bilateral governmental loans and publicly guaranteed supplier credits.   Credits with maturities under 180 days, all commercial bank credits and all loans from international financial institutions (World Bank, regional development banks) as well as debts between LDCs are excluded from this table.

Source: Robert N. Bee, "Lessons from Debt Reschedulings in the Past," *Euromoney*, April 1977, pp. 33-36.

The recent survey[12] of Association of Reserve City Bankers in March 1977 showed that almost all the member banks utilized formal country exposure reporting procedures, and the majority of responding banks prepared country exposure reports monthly. Only 12 banks (14 percent) with foreign exposure did not prepare country exposure reports on a regular basis. The international assets of these banks were less than 5 percent of their total assets.

Commercial banks could discriminate among LDC borrowers by charging them different interest rates. But because of the rationing process to maximize return subject to a risk constraint, discrimination by interest in the commercial lendings to LDCs is not significant nor consistent enough to identify.[13]

An LDC seeking to borrow without an external commercial borrowings history often can borrow on better terms. A recent case is India which has received bank loans of $50 million over seven years at 1 percent over London interbank offered rates (LIBOR). India has rescheduled its payments to foreign creditors more frequently than any other country during the last ten years. As the loan amount increases, borrowers pay slightly higher interest. Beyond a certain point, a country cannot borrow due to the exposure limit. As a *Euromoney* editorial in October 1977 points out: "From a country borrower's point of view, general economic performance is no longer very important. Nor is its political coloring or government."

This process of rationing makes the country exposure limit, not the interest rate, an important criterion in selecting the loan portfolio in commercial banks. The actual interest rate behavior shows that the difference in the interest spreads between LDCs and developed countries becomes smaller. In addition, the range of spreads among LDCs are so narrow that they can hardly be differentiated. For example, the spreads to LDCs on publicly announced Eurocurrency credits during 1976 ranged only between 1.125 percent and 2.125 percent over LIBOR. Figure 1.1 shows the relationship of interest rates to LDC loans and exposure limits to LDCs.

I. Kapur also explains the rationing of Euromarkets as follows.

(a) If they could, lenders would discriminate among borrowers through interest and noninterest elements in the price of loans, (b) under market conditions where perfect discrimination is not possible, for institutional or other reasonings, while the interest and noninterest price of loans will reflect some of the differences in creditworthiness among borrowers, the allocation of loans will be based on a system of quantity rationing.[14]

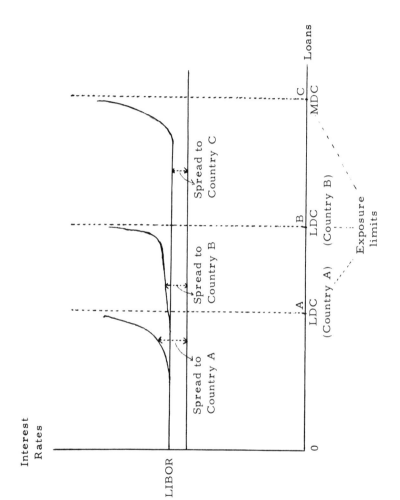

Figure 1-1. Exposure Limits and Interest Rates to LDC Loans.

Theoretical Literature on Rationing

Theoretical frameworks for credit rationing have been developed by D. Hodgman (1960), M. Freimer and H. Goldon (1965), and D. Jaffee and F. Modigliani (1969) (1976). They have shown that rationing is consistent with the rational economic behavior of profit maximization in the presence of uncertainty. Within a risk-return context which does not rely upon oligopolistic market structure or legal maxima to the interest rate, Hodgman[15] asserted that given a risk ratio -- the ratio of the expected value of the payments to the bank to the expected value of the probable losses (including interest payment) -- a banker will refuse to extend credit beyond some level regardless of the interest rate. He explained that there is a positive relationship, *ceteris paribus*, between the size of loan and the risk, the probability of the borrower's inability to repay the loan. He showed that as the amount loaned increases, the risk ratio can be kept above a predetermined figure by increasing the interest rate. Beyond some loan level, however, raising the interest rate will not prevent a fall in the risk ratio. Hodgman's analysis was concerned only with "weak credit rationing." That is, a banker will vary the amount he is willing to lend a borrower with the interest rate up to a limit. Beyond this limit he will refuse to extend credit regardless of the interest rate.[16]

M. Freimer and H. Goldon extended Hodgman's argument more extensively and rigorously. They found that the amount a profit-maximizing banker is willing to lend a borrower is highly interest inelastic. They showed, on the basis of the supplier's loan offer curve,[17] that the optimal amount of high risk loan rises with interest rate but by decreasing amounts up to a limit, whereas the optimal loan is practically independent of the interest rate on low risk loans. Further, they argued that "the interest cost of obtaining additional credit is large, and one wonders who would want much, if any, more credit than the bank would be willing to give at the conventional interest rate."[18] They continue, "for a very wide range of circumstances, we would not observe loans made at rates above the customary rate, because the borrowers would find the interest elasticity of the amount the banker is willing to lend too low."[19]

Recently, C. Azzi and J. Cox[20] raised a question on the credit rationing argument which is based only on the interest rate. They considered how borrower-provided collateral (or equity) affects the incentive of lenders to ration credit through non-price means. They developed a series of propositions which show that the larger the amount of borrower-provided collateral, the greater the size of the loan supplied by the lender.

In a reply on their argument, D. Jaffee and F. Modigliani agreed that "the provision of borrower collateral is tantamount to a shift toward a less risky investment project for the lender."[21] "Moreover, in the limit there is a sufficient amount of collateral to eliminate the risk of default entirely, and then no rationing can occur. On the other hand, if less collateral than this amount is provided, then there is a residual risk of default and credit rationing remains a possibility."[22] Even when the borrower chooses the optimal amount of collateral, credit rationing can occur if lenders cannot freely discriminate between borrowers on their collateral requirements. It is because the condition of imperfect discrimination on collateral requirements parallels the condition of imperfect discrimination on interest charges, on which Jaffee and Modigliani developed a theoretical framework.

In summary, the primary point of the theoretical argument for credit rationing is that lenders either maximize return subject to a risk constraint or maximize a joint function of return and risk.[23]

NOTES

[1]For a detailed study of the development of supplier credits see IMF, "The Use of Commercial Credits by Developing Countries for Financing Imports of Capital Goods," 1968.

[2]Those countries whose estimated per capita income level in 1970 was less than $1,000 (U.S.).

[3]The difference between a syndicated credit and a direct commercial loan is that in the syndicated credit a number of banks participate at the outset.   The reasons for development of the syndicated Eurocredits are:

    (1)   the need and the increasing size of loan demand,
    (2)   the need to spread the risks,
    (3)   the attractiveness of management fees,
    (4)   the publicity for participating banks, and
    (5)   the desire to form profitable working relationships with other banks.

See Robert N. Bee, "Syndication," in *Offshore Lending by U.S. Commercial Banks* edited by F. John Mathis (Washington, D.C.: Bankers' Association for Foreign Trade and Robert Morris Associates, 1975), pp. 151-152.

[4]Ian H. Giddy and Russ Ray, "The Eurodollar Market and the Third World," *Business Review* (The University of Michigan), March 1976, p. 12.

[5]Andrew F. Brimmer, "International Capital Markets and the Financing of Economic Development," Paper presented as the inaugural lecture in the Samuel Z. Westerfield, Jr., Distinguished Lecture Series, Atlanta University, 1973, pp. 18-20.

[6]Azizali F. Mohammed and Fabrizio Saccomanni, "Short-Term Banking and Euro-Currency Credits to Developing Countries," *International Monetary Fund Staff Papers*, November 1973, pp. 612-638.

[7]Andrew Liddell, "Syndicated Eurocredits: The Drift Towards The Big Banks," *The Banker*, November 1976, p. 1221.

[8]Since 1973 IBRD has used the "twin" criteria of (1) access to private capital markets and (2) the level of per capita income ($1,000 per capita income level in 1970 prices) to judge whether a country should be phased out of the bank lending.   While the argument for the adoption of a relative rather than a fixed income criterion exists (the relative income criterion in terms of the average income of the OECD "North" countries composed of U.S., U.K., France, Germany, Japan, Belgium and Netherlands), the access to private capital markets at reasonable terms remains the most important criterion.

The access to external capital markets, however, has been determined subjectively by factors such as the country's level of economic and social development; its natural and human resource endowment; its growth record and prospects; the quality of its economic management; the nature of its trade links; and its geo-political situation. There has been no objective formula to determine whether a country is likely to have adequate access to private capital on reasonable terms.

[9]Antoine W. van Agtmael, "Evaluating the risks of lending to developing countries," *Euromoney*, April 1976, p. 16.

[10]According to the 1977 survey of the Association of Reserve City Bankers, the determination of what is included as *country exposure* and how this exposure is disaggregated is a function of two principal factors: (1) the materiality in volume terms of particular types of assets and off-balance sheet transactions to a given bank's operation, and (2) the information requests from regulatory authorities, Boards of Directors, internal auditors, etc.

As a general rule, banks include most balance sheet items such as loans, advances, overdrafts and also certain types of off-balance sheet items such as contingent liabilities (clean, and standby letter of credit, formal but unutilized commitments to lend). There is, however, less consistency in the treatment of balance sheet items such as placements with foreign branches and/or subsidiaries of third party banks, of contingent liabilities arising from forward exchange contracts, intra-bank placements, and of other risk assets such as shipping loans supported by various charter party assignments.

[11]A. Bruce Brackenridge, "Evaluating Country Credits," *Institutional Investors*, June 1977, p. 13. Brackenridge, senior vice president of Morgan Guaranty Trust Co., was a member of a task force in 1977 to survey the definitions and computational procedures employed by member banks of Association of Reserve City Bankers in quantifying country exposure.

[12]Association of Reserve City Bankers, *Country Exposure Measurement and Reporting Practices of Members Bankers*, March 1977.

[13]Refer to the more detailed explanation presented in Chapter II.

[14]Isham Kapur, "An Analysis of the Supply of Euro-Currency Finance to Developing Countries," *Oxford Bulletin of Economics and Statistics*, August 1977, p. 177.

[15]Donald R. Hodgman, "Credit Risk and Credit Rationing," *Quarterly Journal of Economics*, May 1960, pp. 258-278.

[16]Marshall Freimer and Myron J. Gordon, "Why Bankers Ration Credit," *Quarterly Journal of Economics*, August 1965, pp. 397-416.

[17]D. Jaffe and F. Modigliani (1969) devised a theoretical model considering three elements, *the demand for loans, the supply of loans,* and *the determinants of the commercial loan rate*, and showed that equilibrium rationing -- credit rationing which occurs when the loan rate is set at its long-run equilibrium level -- is rational economic behavior of commercial banks. Previous studies concentrated on the determinants of the quantity supplied by lenders while neglecting the other two elements, the demand for loans and the determinants of the commercial loan rate.

[18]M. Freimer and H. Goldon, op. cit., p. 405.

[19]Ibid., p. 413.

[20]Carry F. Azzi and James C. Cox, "A Theory and Test of Credit Rationing: Comment," *The American Economic Review*, December 1976, pp. 911-915.

[21]Dwight M. Jaffee and Franco Modigliani, "A Theory and Test of Credit Rationing: Reply," *The American Economic Review*, December 1976, p. 919.

[22]Ibid., p. 919.

[23]Benjamin M. Friedman, "Credit Rationing: A Review," *Staff Economic Studies*, No. 72, Board of Governors of the Federal System, 1972, p. 15.

CHAPTER II

EMPIRICAL STUDIES ON CREDITWORTHINESS OF LDCs

Method of Conventional Credit Analysis

According to a recent survey[1] of U.S. banks by Export-Import Bank of the United States concerning the techniques used to assess the country risk, there are few attempts to devise a reliable statistical method of identifying debt servicing difficulties. The reasons are explained in the previous chapter. Most banks' evaluations are based on the qualitative analysis or the index system.

The qualitative analysis is generally used by banks as an intermediate method preceding development of a more structured system. The index system centers around the evaluation report of the individual country which contains all the information necessary to review the country's economic, political, and social conditions and prospects. The information is gathered from numerous primary and secondary sources by headquarters line personnel responsible for preparing the evaluation. The country evaluation report follows no standardized format, however, and, as a result, they vary in depth and scope from country to country. Although it permits the evaluation to focus on each country's unique attributes and possible problem areas, it creates difficulty in comparing countries systematically.[2]

The index system assigns a rating to each country with respect to predetermined indicators. The indicators are proxy variables for factors which include everything necessary and available to judge the creditworthiness of the present and future economic and political conditions of the country. The typical examples of these factors are the country's level of economic and social development, balance-of-payment trends, external debt structures and service requirements, natural and human resource endowment, external debt management, and other political variables.

The mechanics of constructing a country risk index vary widely from bank to bank.[3] The indicators and weights thereon are subjectively determined by banks based on their historical experiences. The common indicators are almost all known, such as, debt service ratio, the level of reserves, debt to GNP ratio. While these indicators have shortcomings[4] when they are used alone (D. Avramovic, et al. (1964), B. Friscia (1973), P. Nagy (1976), D. Duff and I. Peacock (1977), I. Friedman (1977), G. Dufey and S. Min (1977), D. Beck (1977), Y. Maroni (1977)), the joint use of several indicators might reduce the shortcomings of individual indicators and help to devise a more reliable method of assessing creditworthiness.

The index system is a more objective criterion than the qualitative analysis in differentiating the creditworthiness among the countries. But because of subjective judgment in determining the indicators and their weights, the index score derived by this method is, inevitably, subjective. According to the Export-Import Bank survey, none of the banks using this method places primary reliance on it; all use the index as a supplement to other qualitative analyses. The predictive power of this index method in assessing the difficulties of debt servicing is also reported to be very insignificant in the survey.

Method of Statistical Credit Analysis

There are two categories of empirical studies: (1) studies based on the actual reschedulings[5] and (2) studies adopting a certain proxy for dependent variable, creditworthiness.

Studies based on rescheduling. In this category are three major studies: C. Frank and W. Cline (1971), P. Dhonte (1975) and by G. Feder and R. Just (1977). The first two studies were prepared by international financial institutions.

By discriminant analysis (multivariate statistical analysis), C. Frank and W. Cline[6] analyzed data for 26 countries including eight that have been rescheduled 13 times over the nine-year period 1960-1968. The authors did not indicate how the 26 countries were chosen or why certain rescheduled countries were excluded from the observations.[7] They did mention, however, that the absence of data for specific years reduced the observations from a maximum of 234 (26 countries x 8 years) to 145 observations, including the 13 observations of rescheduled countries.

Frank and Cline sought an index or indicator of the likelihood that a country would experience debt servicing difficulties. Their criteria for selecting the indicator were simplicity and a high degree of predictability. "To obtain some notion of the relative importance of the variables," they performed a linear regression test[8] and found that three of eight indicators in the model were significant at the 5 percent level.

Using iterated linear discriminant functions they tested whether the selected three variables -- ratio of debt service to export, debt amortization to total outstanding debt (the inverse of the "average" maturity of loans), and ratio of imports to reserves -- had the ability to predict debt rescheduling.[9] They ran a ratio of imports to reserves, with and without the variable, based on their sample data set. They found that by estimating quadratic functions as well as linear functions it was possible to obtain "a very high prediction rate" by using only two indicators, the debt service ratio, and ratio of debt amortization to the total debt outstanding. During the period 1960-1968, the linear function using these two indicators correctly predicted 12 of the 13 reschedulings, but also predicted 17 reschedulings which did not occur. However, 13 of these 17 errors were for observations from countries which in nearby years did in fact have reschedulings.

P. Dhonte[10] analyzed a control group of 69 countries as well as the 11 countries with 13 reschedulings during the period 1959-1971. He used both individual indicator analysis and principal-component analysis to investigate what was distinctive about these countries' cases compared with a control group of 69 countries. A certain individual indicator could differentiate the rescheduling cases from the average of the sample of 69 countries. Typical features of the rescheduling case were: (1) a high level of debt; (2) a high level of debt service payments; (3) bunching, that is, a large portion of scheduled service payments on existing obligations fell due within the next few years; and (4) a strong dependence on capital inflows in relation to imports. These features confirm our general understanding of the liquidity problem.

The other important finding of the individual indicator analysis was that the ratio of average annual debt service payments to exports -- an average over a selected period or as a sum of discounted debt service payment over the period, which are then divided by current export values -- in time (t-1) was, in all instances (except one) lower for the renegotiation cases than the average ratio of the sample control group countries, while the renegotiation cases as a whole displayed high debt service ratios which accounted for only current debt service payments. This indicates that, while a high level of debt service payments is a phenomenon accompanying rescheduling, rescheduling cannot be anticipated on the basis of only the prior year ratio of average annual debt service payments to exports. One must also evaluate the bunching of debt service obligations. One conclusion of this individual indicator analysis is that the predictive power of these indicators is weak and that "the renegotiation cases, which appeared as examples of high debt-service obligations at the time of the renegotiation, did not appear as such in longer-range perspective."

Principal-components approach, the analysis of relationships among various indicators, revealed that renegotiations were necessary when a balance was not maintained (1) between the extent of involvement in debt and the terms (borrowing conditions), and (2) between the growth of debt and the growth of exports. Although this approach correctly predicted 10 of 12 renegotiation cases at the *one standard deviation* significance level, it also predicted eight cases in which renegotiation did not in fact take place. On the basis of this test result, we can conclude that this study suggests a rough indication of emerging debt difficulties but fails to provide a reliable forecasting tool.

The objective of the rescheduling study done by G. Feder and R. Just[11] was the same as the previous two studies: investigating the importance of various economic factors in determining debt servicing capacity of borrowing countries. Instead of discriminant or principal component analyses, however, they used logit analysis. They argued, "Logit analysis is used instead of discriminant analysis because it is a method specifically developed to deal with the binary-valued, dependent-variable case. While discriminant analysis assumes two completely different populations, the logit approach assumes a discrete 'event' takes place after the combined effect of certain economic variables reaches some threshold level."[12]

They analyzed data for 41 countries (238 observations) including the 11 rescheduled countries (21 observations) over eight years, 1967 to 1972. Data relating to years preceding 1967 were not considered because of non-availability from public sources. They found that six variables were significantly related to debt serving capacity. In addition to the ratios of debt service to export, debt amortization to total outstanding debt, and imports to reserves (suggested by the Frank and Cline results), they found three other variables to be important indicators of debt servicing capacity: export growth rate, per capita income, and ratio of capital inflows to debt service. They argued that, because these variables included indicators of short as well as long-term capacity, "the probability of default thus appears to depend not only on the circumstances prevailing immediately before the year on which a forecast is being made but also on trends based on a relatively long period of time preceding the forecast."[13]

The predictive performance of the estimates was quite good within the observation periods; there were no more than 11 errors in a total of 238 observations.

Major findings of three studies based on rescheduling are summarized in Table 2-1.

Studies adopting a certain proxy for dependent variables. Some studies consider the interest rate as the proxy for the dependent variable, creditworthiness. The rationales are that in the competitive international capital market, the creditworthiness of a borrower is reflected in the price of funds, the interest rate, and that other elements of the total cost of funds, such as repayment terms and maturities, are not the result of risk perceptions of the bank regarding the individual borrowers so much as the overall state of the market. In this vein, H. Cleveland and B. Brittain[14] (1977) regressed debt/income ratios over the three years 1974-

Table 2-1

A Summary of Empirical Studies Based on Reschedulings

	Frank & Cline (1971)	Dhonte (1975)	Feder & Just (1977)
Purpose of study	To find an indicator to predict debt servicing difficulties	To investigate the relationships among ratios to provide a description of debt situation.	To investigate the importance of economic factors in determining debt servicing capacity.
Method of study	Discriminant analysis	Principal-component analysis and individual ratio analysis	Logit analysis
Data period	1960-1968	1959-1971	1965-1972
Number of reschedulings included (see Appendix I)	13	13	21
Total observations	145	234	238
Explanatory variables in the model	(1) Debt service/exports (2) Growth rate of exports (3) Export fluctuation index (4) Non-compressible imports (5) Per capita income (6) Debt amortization/total outstanding debt (7) Imports/GNP (8) Imports/reserves	(1) Reserves/debt outstanding (2) Debt service/disbursements (3) Debt service ratio (4) Debt service/debt outstanding (5) Debt outstanding/exports (6) Debt outstanding/GNP (7) Growth rate of debt (8) Growth rate of exports (9) Net transfers/imports	(1) Debt service/exports (2) Growth rate of exports (3) Export fluctuation index (4) Per capita income (5) Debt amortization/total outstanding debt (6) Imports/GNP (7) Imports/reserves (8) GDP growth rate

Table 2-1 (Continued)

	Frank & Cline (1971)	Dhonte (1975)	Feder & Just (1977)
Significant variables (test result)	(1) Debt service/exports (2) Debt amortization to total outstanding (3) Imports/reserves	(10) Disbursements/imports (1) Relationship between the extent of involvement in debt and the terms (2) Relationship between the growth of debt and the growth of exports	(9) Capital inflow/debt service (1) Debt service/exports (2) Debt amortization to total outstanding (3) Imports/reserves
Predictability	Type I error: 0-8 Type II error: 12-26 (out of 145 observations)	Not applicable	Type I error: 0-3 Type II error: 1-11 (out of 238 observations)

1976 against the interest rate spreads over LIBOR on publicly announced Eurocurrency credits to LDCs to determine which indicator was the major determinant of interest rates on LDC loans. They chose debt (income ratio) as the explanatory variable on the a priori grounds that "income provides a better measure of the flow of revenues that could ultimately be garnered for debt service payment if ever the need arose, than do other measures such as exports which measure foreign exchange earnings under normal conditions."[15]

The test showed a statistically significant correlation between interest spreads and debt/income ratios for the years, 1975 and 1976 (r^2 = .5138), which implied that the creditworthiness of a country depended upon the debt/income ratio, among others.

Another case for using interest rate as proxy is to determine whether commercial banks have compensated adequately for the additional risks incurred in lending to LDCs and whether there are variations within the group of developing countries.[16] N. Sargen (1976) used the spread over LIBOR as a dependent variable and performed a regression for the one year period from March 1974. He found that the spread was a function of income level, inflation rate, and debt/service ratio.

Using interest rate as a proxy variable for creditworthiness leaves some unsolved questions. First, the publicized interest rate to LDCs is not the effective cost to those borrowers. The publicized interest rate is only a nominal cost which is a part of a variety of other costs. These hidden costs are hard to determine because they are packaged in the loan agreement and subsequent memoranda in such a manner that outsiders can hardly single them out. This is how bankers differentiate a homogeneous commodity.

The unpublicized costs, in case of the syndicated credit, include fees and commissions to the lead bank and participating banks in the form of management fee, participating fee, and commitment fee. When LDC borrowers are presented with an interest spread over LIBOR, and front-end fee which covers all fees and commissions, the effective cost is not difficult to be derived. In many cases, however, these fees and commissions are neither clear-cut nor known to the public.

The second argument is that the interest rate to LDCs is determined not only by demand conditions, but also by supply conditions. Thus the simple cross-section analysis cannot distinguish interest rate differences resulting from the market condition. B. Quinn (1975) and S. Davis (1977) argue that the tiering of LIBOR rates is also influenced by the supply conditions of the capital markets. For example, the recent sluggish investment to inventory and capital assets in the developed countries and reduced funding demanded by multinational firms have induced banks to maintain loanable funds that are too large.

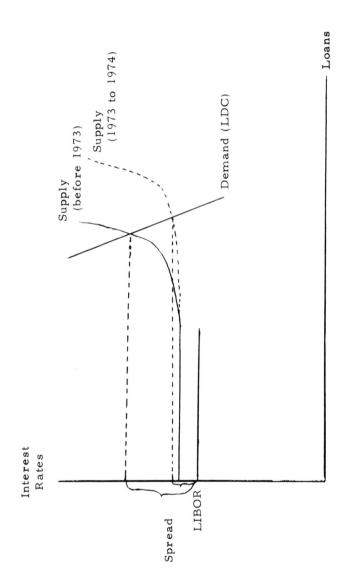

Figure 2-1. Effects of Supply Condition on the Interest Rate to LDCs.

Thus, since 1973 the LDC borrowers have been able to obtain funds easily at the better terms compared to previous years.

A third argument is that loans to LDCs are determined through the informal system of credit rationing. Banks allocate exposure limits depending on the creditworthiness of countries. Theoretical frameworks for credit rationing of commercial banks have been reviewed in Chapter I. The major points of the argument are that bankers refuse to extend credit beyond some level regardless of the interest rate, and that this rationing is consistent with rational economic behavior of profit maximization in the presence of uncertainty. This theoretical argument has been supported by the recent survey taken by Export-Import Bank of the United States on the international lending practices of commercial banks. The results of the survey reveal that "many of the banks use the results from the country evaluation system in setting maximum exposure limits; a few banks use the results to help analyze the quality of their portfolio. None of the respondent banks use the results in fixing interest rates or fees."[17]

As M. Freimer and M. Gordon mentioned, we can note "that there will be some variation in the interest rates charged by bankers which behave in this way due to the bargaining by customers for lower interest rates, the variation in the non-interest cost of lending among borrowers, and the borrower who insists (often because the immediate threat of insolvency leaves him no choice) on more credit than he can obtain at the customary rate."[18] By referring to theoretical arguments and actual practice, however, we can conclude that credit rationing is an actual behavior of commercial bankers in the international lending.

Along the lines of this credit rationing argument, I. Kapur[19] tested the supply of Eurocurrency credit to LDCs. He asserted that "the amounts rationed are dependent upon perceptions of selective creditworthiness of borrowers," and "that when banks cannot discriminate among borrowers through the cost of funds due to the liquidity of interest rates, bankers allocate funds to LDCs on the basis of quantity rationing." He used cross-section regression analysis on data from 25 LDCs which borrowed from the Eurocurrency markets during the period 1972-1974. The major determinants of supply of credit, indirectly the creditworthiness, turned out to be the current level and expected growth of exports, the overall growth performance of the economy, and the projected change in debt-service relative to export receipts. The existing level of bank commitment of borrowers was negatively related to supply of new credit.

The purpose of this study was to test empirically the factors underlying the supply of Eurocurrency finance to LDCs. Thus the construction of the explanatory variables was done without a theoretical framework explaining why particular variables were chosen, and the study used a limited number of explanatory variables excluding variables indicating political stability or willingness to pay. However, this study is the initial one, and the rationing approach of the study sheds light on the possibility of evaluation of creditworthiness.

NOTES

[1]See Stephen Goodman, "How the Big U.S. Banks Really Evaluate Sovereign Risk," *Euromoney*, February 1977, and Export-Import Bank of the Unitd States (Policy Analysis Staff), "A Survey of Country Evaluation Systems in Use," December 22, 1976.

[2]Ibid., Export-Import Bank of the United States, p. 10.

[3]For example, the Bank of America country risk rating system related to credit, investment and liability exposure utilizes two criteria: (1) an adaptability index, and (2) the external debt servicing index.

The adaptability index measures how well a country's economy can adapt to changing environmental conditions. Eight economic variables are used in the adaptability index: real gross domestic product per capita (30%), consumer prices (15%), merchandise export earnings (15%), domestic and foreign savings (10%), exchange rate adjustment (5%), and IMF account position (5%). The figures within the parentheses are weights of those variables.

The external debt servicing index attempts to measure the relationship between a country's projected service on its external debt and the resources that are available for that service. Four economic variables and their weights in the external debt servicing index are as follows: external debt servicing capacity ratio (50%), months of imports covered (20%), total external debt divided by GNP (20%), and a compressibility ratio (10%).

For more details, see Richard Puz, "How to Find Out When a Sovereign Borrower Slips from A-1 to C-3," *Euromoney*, December 1977, pp. 67-71, and "Techniques of Credit Rating: BOA Methodology," *Asian Finance*, 15 September/14 October 1977, pp. 46-47.

[4]These indicators provide the banks with useful information on the external debt situation of a country.   If these are used mechanically without considering other criteria, these indicators have the capacity to mislead.   Due to the limitations of these indicators, we cannot judge whether a country with a poor ratio is necessarily a bad credit risk if it has good growth expectations for its exports and overall economy, and vice versa.   For example, the most widely used indicator, the debt service ratio, has some shortcomings: (1) The ratio underestimates the total debt servicing burden because it does not take into account servicing on short-term debt and on long-term private debt that is not publicly guaranteed; (2) there is no clear maximum acceptable level for the ratio other than that default is probable.   The maximum acceptable level was widely believed to be around 20 percent. Yet, Mexico has continuously borrowed for many years with a debt service ratio of around 30 percent without experiencing serious debt service difficulties, while Indonesia with a ratio of 10 percent was compelled to request the rescheduling of external debts.   During the 1950s Japan had high debt service ratios, but excellent growth record and economic management made the country quite creditworthy.   In the 1930s Australia also had a debt service ratio of 44 percent and avoided default; (3) the ratio is computed on the basis of actual disbursed service payments, not on the basis of payment due.   Thus if a country is unable to meet its debt serving obligations, the ratio can drop in spite of deteriorating debt servicing conditions.

[5]"Consolidations" might be a more appropriate term here since the empirical studies are based on consolidation rather than rescheduling. In the original IBRD-DAC terminology under the Expanded Reporting System, three types of debt refunding -- the direct debt relief method -- were specified: (1) rescheduling, (2) refinancing, and (3) consolidation. H. Bittermann (1973) distinguishes these three types of refunding as follows:

Rescheduling, especially in the case of foreign private obligors, refers to the debt relief method in which debt payment is postponed by amendment of the terms of individual loan contracts. There is no cancellation of principal, generally no change in interest rates, but merely a reduction of the principal payments in the course of a year or number of years. In the case of private loans this may be practically necessary when the original loan contract provided for a definite schedule of repayment through a series of notes, but delays in the construction or other factors make it impossible for the obligor to repay according to the original schedule.

Refinancing applies to loans whereby an offical agency "takes over" credits previously extended by private creditors. Often this involves trade credits or suppliers credits to the government or private business entities in the debt country which had been guaranteed or insured by a public body in either the creditor or debtor country. The devices used by various countries differ, and many of the "consolidations" (see below) have been partly "refinancing."

Consolidation is a rescheduling of maturities used to fund arrears or future payments, as they fall due, of principal or interest on loans previously made by the same public creditor or group of creditors. The consolidation may involve cancelling outstanding credits and instituting a new credit instrument with a new schedule of interest and maturity. The consolidation may be bilateral or multilateral. For more detail, see Henry J. Bittermann, *The Refunding of International Debt*, 1973, pp. 77-78.

[6]Charles R. Frank, Jr., and William R. Cline, "Measurement of Debt Servicing Capacity: An Application of Discriminant Analysis," *Journal of International Economics*, No. 1, 1971, pp. 327-344.

[7]The eight countries included in the analysis were Argentina, Brazil, Chile, Ghana, India, Indonesia, Turkey, and the U.A.R. Among the other coutries which also were rescheduled during the sample period were Liberia, Mali, the Philippines, Peru, Uruguay, Yugoslavia. These were not included in the observations.

[8]The equation used was $Y_t = \beta_0 + \beta_x$ where $Y_t = 1$ if the tth observation came from rescheduling sample population and $Y_t = 0$ if from nonrescheduling sample population.

[9]G. Feder and R. Just argue that "the testing procedure used in the Frank and Cline study may not be valid for two reasons. First, 't' and 'F' tests are not quite legitimate measures for discriminant analysis because of normality assumptions. Second, even if these tests were legitimate, the F test should be used to test whether several variables are unimportant simultaneously." See G. Feder and R. Just, "A Study of Debt Servicing Capacity Applying Logit Analysis," p. 26.

CHAPTER III

MODEL AND METHOD OF THE STUDY

Assumptions

As mentioned in the previous chapter, there have been few serious attempts to devise a reliable statistical method of evaluating creditworthiness. The four most important studies addressing credit-worthiness are those by C. Frank and W. Cline, P. Dhonte, C. Feder and R. Just, and I. Kapur. The first two studies (applying discriminant analysis and principal-components analysis) suggest a rough indicator of the likelihood that a country would experience debt servicing difficulties, but they failed to provide a strong statistical indicator on which to rely. The study of F. Feder and E. Just provided better estimates. The predictive performances of the estimates were valid for the limited sample included in their study.

All these studies are limited to formal multilateral rescheduling cases of bilateral governmental loans and public guaranteed supplier credit (see Appendix 1), primarily because no similar data are available on obligations to private lenders such as commercial banks.[1] There also have been many indirect refunding arrangements for borrowings from private lenders, the effects of which have been similar to those of formal multilateral reschedulings in reducing difficulties resulting from (foreign exchange) cash flow problems. As LDCs have borrowed more from private lenders, the importance of these indirect refunding arrangements has increased. "Roll-over" is one of these arrangements. S. Davis explicitly mentions that "Following the heavy country borrowings of the early 1970s, a large number of LDCs are now dependent on the Euromarkets to roll over existing obligations, ..."[2] Thus the studies excluding these refunding arrangements on the borrowings from the private lenders have only a limited use, even in evaluating the short-term difficulties resulting from cash-flow problems.

Even if the evaluations based on reschedulings were reliable in predicting debt servicing difficulties, this does not necessarily imply that they measure the creditworthiness of a country because short-term difficulties usually result from the cash flow problem rather than the country's inability to create additional output sufficient to cover the costs for input and debt service.

The study by Kapur provides a starting point for the study I propose. It incorporates two underlying assumptions: (1) Euro-banks lending to LDCs are more likely to differentiate countries by country exposure limit; and (2) there is always an excess individual country demand for funds at any given price prevailing in Euromarkets.

Excess Demand for Funds

Economic development has been a vital theme of all LDCs, and capital has been regarded as central to the process of economic development. As indicated by S. Kuznets,[3] based on experiences of developed countries, the absorptive capacity[4] -- technical, human, and social capacity to transform investments into real investments -- is a prerequisite to secure development. His empirical test showed that the direct contribution of capital accumulation and man-hours accounted for a fraction of total growth in GNP and that factors, such as improved quality of the resources, managerial capacity, technical change, accounted for the remaining portion of total growth. But no one argues that capital formation is still the single main factor in the development process of LDCs.

The ultimate capital accumulation required for development is the extent to which a country can transform the economy in a way that permanently increases its ability to contribute to its economic welfare. In a static society where people are unconcerned with raising their standard of living, new capital for investment may not be necessary. Thus capital requirements depend on a country's target rate of investment which is determined by the target rate of growth. Most LDCs have been eager to develop their countries to the extent that the investment requirements reach beyond their savings potential. Thus they experience a shortage of capital.

The capital requirements must be financed as long as a country wishes to attain its development target. Since LDCs do not have enough domestic savings to fill their capital requirements, this "savings gap" should be filled by external sources. This gap is reflected in the current account deficit of the balance of payments and is filled by reduction in the reserves and/or the transferred capital, which consists of net flows of grants, direct investments, portfolio investments, suppliers credits, or borrowings.

As mentioned in Chapter I, since 1973-74 non-oil producing LDCs' foreign exchange requirements have exceeded what they were likely to obtain from their traditional sources. Consequently, LDCs have had to rely on commercial banks for their remaining requirements. But because of the credit rationing behavior of commercial banks, beyond a certain point (the exposure limit) would-be LDC borrowers were not able to borrow at any rates of interest. Thus there was an excess demand for funds from LDCs in the private capital markets.

Even though some LDCs have not tried to enter private capital markets, this is not because they have not needed external capital for development. Rather, they have not had capacity, or creditworthiness, to borrow in private capital markets and/or they could not find an investment project whose return would exceed the cost of borrowing.

Based on these two assumptions, i.e., credit rationing and excess demand of LDCs for funds, the loan amounts from the private capital market, adjusted for differences in external capital requirements between countries, will be used as the proxy for creditworthiness in this study. The loan amounts from the private source will be divided by the external financing requirements (need)[5] of a country (loan amounts ÷ needs) so that the dependent variable will be the creditworthiness index of a country and will range between one and zero value.

External Financing Requirements (Need)

The current account deficit. The current account deficit of the balance of payments may be used as a proxy for the external financing requirement. In this case, the index of creditworthiness will represent a private financing proportion of the total external financing. Because the current account deficit is the actual figure representing what was the external financing requirement of a country, it has the merit of objectivity. But the actual current account deficit which already has been adjusted for financing constraints does not match the initial external financing requirement, anticipated based on the "aimed" economic development target. The credit rationing behavior of commercial banks has prevented would-be LDC borrowers from borrowing as much as they would like at market rates of interest. In addition, certain LDCs have not been able to find projects which yield more than interest cost of borrowings from private capital markets. Thus such unsatisfied LDC borrowers had to choose between either cutting back on their development plans or resort to belt-tightening policies, reducing current consumption. As a result, the ex post current account deficit cannot be a reliable proxy for the external financing requirement.

Estimation of the capital requirements. The estimate of capital requirements can be derived by the aggregate investment requirement method and the project-by-project method. The aggregate investment method is based on the Harrod-Domar model,[6] which assesses the capital requirement based on a target of growth rate, savings ratio, and capital-output ratio. It begins by setting a target rate of income growth which is to be the goal of the country, then estimates the amount of capital to achieve that target based on capital-output relationships. This approach has been used in the United Nations studies on the capital requirement estimate of LDCs as the basis of the presentation made to the first and second UNCTAD conferences. On the other hand, the World Bank

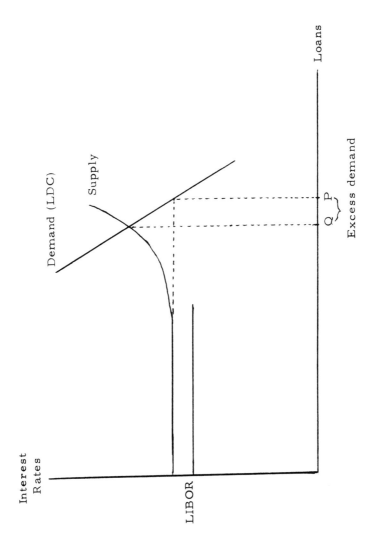

Figure 3-1. Excess Demand of LDCs for Funds

Group adopted the second method. Instead of using an explicit overall target, they estimate an overall requirement from a multidimensional examination of the economy in question by estimating project-by-project or sector-by-sector requirements.[7] The aggregate investment requirement method of the Harrod-Domar model is more appropriate for this study because the estimation of capital requirements can be based on the known factors which can be put into quantitative terms.

The concept of the capital-output ratio in the model is the broad concept of incremental capital-output ratio (ICOR) which is "a comparison of the output that could be obtained with or without the added capital, but with other inputs adapted to work most efficiently with the specified added amount of capital, at any given time."[8] Thus the ratio carries within it all of the factors affecting growth of output: investment, natural resources, technology, the availability of labor, and management skills. The savings ratio is the ratio of national savings (S) which is different from the domestic savings by investment income payments abroad. Target investment (I*) is the target gross domestic investment.

Based on these concepts, the external financing requirement (R) can be presented in the following formula:

$$R = I^* - S$$

Since $I^* = GDP \times g^* \times ICOR$, or $Y \cdot \dfrac{\Delta Y}{Y} \cdot \dfrac{\Delta K}{\Delta Y}$,

$$R = GDP (g^* \times ICOR - s), \text{ or } Y(\frac{\Delta Y}{Y} \cdot \frac{\Delta K}{\Delta Y} - s) \qquad (1)$$

where g^* = target income growth rate

        s = national average savings rate

       Y = GDP

       K = capital

In other words, the external financing requirement is a function of level of income, target income growth rate, incremental capital-output ratio, and national savings ratio. Level of income, incremental capital-output ratio, and national savings ratio are the known factors for a given country in a given time period. However, unless a country accepts some given national savings rate as optimum and then plan its growth with that savings potential, the income growth target is determined by the external financing availability. The external financing requirement can be regarded as "a missing element required to permit a larger investment than would be possible given the domestic factor availabilities, local infrastructure, and the savings possibilities opened up by the policies and level of performance of the government."[9]

If a country cannot obtain financing from external sources, it has to satisfy itself by limiting its growth target within the country's savings potential (intrinsic growth rate). Some countries may try to develop their countries within their savings potential. If, however, every LDC wants economic development as rapidly as possible, it will have to borrow externally as much as possible to the extent that it can find an investment project the return on which exceeds the cost of borrowing. In this sense, the target rate will be infinite within the constraints of the absorptive capacity of the country and the availability of the investment projects.

Since the external financing requirement in the model refers to external financing requirements from private sources, the other financing sources which could fill the requirements -- foreign direct investment, aid, loans from governments and loans from international organizations -- will be excluded. As a result, the needs will be modified to be the external financing needed from private sources (RC), and its equation will be as follows:

$$RC = GDP(g^* \cdot ICOR - s - p) \qquad (2)$$

where p = the ratio of total amounts financing from the public sources to GDP

Thus the creditworthiness index (Q ÷ Needs) can be transformed in the following equation:

Since Q = I - S - P,

$$Q = GDP(g \cdot ICOR - s - p) \qquad (3)$$

where g   = actual income growth rate

P   = total amounts financing from the public sources

From equations (2) and (3),

$$\frac{Q}{Needs} = \frac{g(ICOR) - s - p}{g^*(ICOR) - s - p} \qquad (4)$$

How can we correctly measure the target rates for the individual countries? This may not be possible. As an alternative, the same target growth rate can be applied to all LDCs because the same opportunity for development should be given to all the LDCs. The question is what target rate should be applied. This is important because the index value of creditworthiness in the model changes depending upon the target rate. In equation (4), the actual income growth rate (g), national savings rate (s), and a portion of external financing from the public sources to GDP (p) are variables which are different depending upon a country and a time period (year). However, the target growth rate (g*) will be constant to all countries and time periods. So the higher the target growth rates, the lower the values of indices for the countries which borrowed less from the private capital markets. This is a result of the characteristics of the incremental capital-output ratio (ICOR) which is greater than 1 for all the countries. For example, if the target growth rate is set 1 percent higher, the effect on the denominator of the creditworthiness index, or needs, is always greater than 1 percent; likewise the reduction effect of the index value is more than 1 percent. The effect of the target growth rate will not be significant on the value of the creditworthiness index if ICORs do not differ between countries. If ICORs differ, however, the value of creditworthiness index will change in favor of countries with lower ICORs. (Nonetheless this bias is in the proper direction.) In other words, the creditworthiness index in this model is influenced by growth and productivity of capital; thus it assigns higher values to those countries with higher income growth and higher productivity of capital.

What should be the target income growth rate? Because the assumption of this study is that every LDC wants economic development as rapidly as possible and that rapid development is constrained by whether it can find the investment project which yields more than the cost of borrowing, the target growth rate for this study is assumed the highest actual growth rate of all LDCs during the study periods.

As a result, the external financing requirement from private sources will be calculated as follows:

$$RC = GDP_t \text{ (the highest actual growth rate x}$$
$$(I_{t-1} \div \Delta GDP_t) - s_t - p_t)$$

A lag of one year will be taken in the incremental capital-output ratio, because investment does not give rise to an increase in production capacity until the investment has been completed.[10]

With a given loan level supplied from private sources, the index value of a country is determined in the following way: If a country has a higher savings rate, the index value will be higher, and vice-versa; the lower the ICOR, the higher the index value, and vice-versa; the higher the portion of financing from other sources, the higher the index value, and vice-versa. The first two relationships are self-explanatory. A country with high savings and a low ICOR[11] will have effective access to domestic resources which, in turn, can be reallocated to production competing with exports or imports permitting expansion in exports or a further reduction in imports.   This will increase the capacity of the country to service foreign borrowings.   The third relationship between the index value and the financing source indicates that, given a level of borrowing from private sources, the country with other financing sources will be more creditworthy compared to the country without them.   While a creditworthy country can borrow more from private capital markets, those countries with more diversified financing sources will have flexibility in servicing their obligations from the private sources.[12]

GDP or population have been suggested to be used as a proxy for external financing requirments.   In this case, loan amount scaled by GDP or per capita loan amount from private sources will be the index which determines the creditworthiness of a country.   One assumption of using GDP as proxy for external financing requirement is that countries of the same economic size will need the same level of funding from external financing.   But even among the countries of the same economic size, the needs for external financing differ depending upon their domestic savings potential, the productivity of capital, and the availability of other financing sources.   These differences are not reflected in the index of loan amount scaled by GDP.   The index of per capita loan amount has the same deficiency as does the loan amount scaled by GDP. The difference between the two indices is simply that the per capita loan amount index is a product of loan amount scaled by GDP and per capita GDP of the country as shown below:

$$\text{Loan amount scaled by GDP} = \frac{Q}{GDP}$$

From equation (3),

$$\frac{Q}{GDP} = \frac{GDP(g \cdot ICOR - s - p)}{GDP}$$

$$= g \cdot ICOR - s - p \qquad\qquad (5)$$

$$\text{Per capita loan amount} = \frac{Q}{\text{population}}$$

From equation (3),

$$\frac{Q}{\text{population}} = \frac{GDP(g \cdot ICOR - s - p)}{\text{population}}$$

$$= \text{per capita GDP} \cdot (g \cdot ICOR - s - p) \qquad\qquad (6)$$

Compared to these two indices using GDP and population, the creditworthiness index derived by the Harrod-Domar model is a better index because, given a level of loan to a particular country, the index reflects the savings potential, the productivity of capital, and the availability of other financing sources of the particular country.

Conceptual Framework and Explanatory Variables

Foreign borrowings will be justified to the extent that the marginal product of capital is greater than the marginal interest cost of foreign borrowings. All economic analyses for foreign borrowing such as "cumulative lending hypothesis" (C. Kindleberger, 1973), "foreign borrowing with instability of national income" (P. Bardhan, 1967 and R. Bade, 1972), "foreign borrowing with export revenue uncertainty" (J. McCahe and D. Sibley, 1976), support the conclusion that the optimal foreign borrowing is the point where the marginal product of capital equals the marginal interest cost of foreign borrowings.

Knowing this microeconomic principle, then, how do we assess the debt serving capability of LDCs? An answer for this question can be derived from our practical knowledge of evaluating a firm's creditworthiness. In assessing creditworthiness of a firm, we do not evaluate only its profitability -- the capacity to create additional output which is sufficient to cover costs for input, debt service, and taxes. The theoretical optimal borrowing condition for the borrower cannot necessarily be the sufficient condition for lenders, because the historical and anticipated profits alone do not guarantee uninterrupted debt servicing or freedom from cash flow bottlenecks and unpredictable, temporary fluctuations in earnings. To determine the cash flow and earnings fluctuations, we must evaluate a country's liquidity, debt structure, and coverage ratios in addition to the evaluation of profitability.

This analogy can be applied to LDC loans. In fact, D. Avramovic, et al. (1964), have illustrated what kind of analytical assessment would be helpful to lenders with this kind of analogy. They link the capacity of an LDC to serve its foreign debt with "its performance in output (sales), savings (plough-back of earnings) and developmental return of capital (ratio of profit)."[13]

What differentiates the international lending from the domestic is the sovereignty risk. The sovereignty risk can be divided into two categories: political stability and willingness to pay. The degree of political stability is an important component of creditworthiness because (1) political instability might bring about economic or social discontinuities that would be detrimental to the borrower's economy, and which would, in turn, reduce the capacity to serve debts; (2) political

Table 3-1

Indicators of Creditworthiness

	Financial analysis for a firm*	Economic analysis for a country
Liquidity	Current ratio = $\dfrac{\text{current assets}}{\text{current liabilities}}$	(Change in) Debt service ratio = $\dfrac{\text{debt service}}{\text{exports}}$
	Acid-test ratio = $\dfrac{\text{quick assets}}{\text{current liabilities}}$	Reserves/imports ratio
Debt structure	Total debt/total capitalization or total debt/net worth	Total external outstanding debt/exports
Coverage ratio	The cash flow coverage ratio = $\dfrac{\text{annual cash flow before interest and taxes}}{\text{interest and principal}}$	Debt service payment/ net capital flow
Profitability	Net profit/total assets or net profit/net worth Net profit or sales per employee	Growth in GDP Growth in exports Per capita income (level of development)
Political stability	Not applicable	General strikes, riots, coups, revolutions, etc.
Willingness to pay	Not applicable	Level of external financing to investment Minimum tolerable level of imports (or level of government revenues) to GDP

*An analysis for a municipal unit's creditworthiness (in measuring municipal bond quality) can be similarly applied.

instability might develop forces which would be detrimental to the interest of foreign lenders, such as repudiation of debt or prevention of foreign currency transfer; (3) the international lenders might not be totally familiar with the political and economic systems of the borrowing country, and this unfamiliarity would increase the discount factor of risk.

In international lending, commercial bankers emphasize the importance of a country's willingness to repay. Even when the individual projects are economically feasible enough to permit borrowers to repay their obligations, the government of the country could prevent the borrower from complying with its obligations. Unlike domestic credit, foreign lenders have no resort when a country is not willing to pay its obligations. In fact, the immediate cause for a number of defaults in Eastern Europe during the 1930s was the inability to transfer funds rather than the borrowers' inability to repay their obligations. Many defaults on Latin American obligations in the 1930s were governmental defaults as a consequence of the decrease in government revenues. "The unwillingness of governments to reduce their total expenditures by the amount of the shrinkage of revenues helped prevent a decline of national income proportional to the fall in foreign exchange earnings; and this in turn led to restriction on the convertability of their currencies."[14]

On the other hand, if a country is willing to pay, "a strong government may be able to squeeze domestic consumption to such an extent that debt service poses no problem even if the foreign funds wind up on investments that do not create sufficient additional output."[15] Thus political consideration and willingness to pay are important parameters in the international lendings.

Growth. Per capita income growth and export growth will be used as indicators for growth. The proxies for growth will be the rates of growth per capita GDP and exports over the previous four years. For the long run, the growth of per capita GDP is the only important factor in the creditworthiness of a country. If a country has the ability to maintain the theoretical optimal borrowing conditions -- that is, the marginal product of capital is greater than the marginal interest cost of foreign borrowings -- the investment outcome of foreign capital will be reflected on the income growth. The important factor from the lender's point of view, to use the analogy of the firm, is the ability of the prospective borrower to expand its net income because it is the only real source from which debt service is paid. R. Mikesell explains:

> Over the longer run, if a firm is successful in continually expanding its net income, it will have little difficulty in meeting its interest and amortization obligations and in expanding its total indebtedness. In case of a country, the long-run capacity to service debts to outside

agencies ultimately depends upon two factors: (1) its ability to expand per capita output and investment; and (2) its ability to increase its export earnings in relation to import requirements and service payments on its indebtedness.[16]

The underlying assumption is that the fulfillment of debt service obligations is dependent on the economy's capacity to adjust the claims on total resources, savings, and foreign exchange in any given year and over time so as to release the amount required for debt service.[17] Increased per capita income provides additional resources to satisfy the aspirations of the populace for rising living standards and to meet debt service.

In the process of growth, export capacity is increased both through expansion of the traditional exports sector and by developing new industries. However, reallocation of resources to exports or import-substitution may be temporarily bottlenecked by rigidities in the internal structure as well as external obstacles that cut export growth. Thus, in addition to per capita income growth, export growth is included as an indicator of growth. The export fluctuations, which are generally associated with probabilities of a balance-of-payments crisis, will be reflected indirectly in this export growth. However, the level of exports has a bearing on the liquidity of a country and will be reflected in the indicators of the debt service ratio and the ratio of reserves to imports.

The absolute level of per capita income will be used as a proxy for economic development. The level of economic development is an essential consideration of creditworthiness because it indicates a country's economic capacity and potential to service its debt. Level of development is generally determined by three measures: per capita GDP, a share of manufacturing in GDP, and a literacy rate used together or separately.[18] This study uses per capita GDP because of its handy and wide use, and in spite of its limitation arising from the fact that income distribution is unequal among LDCs and differs substantially from country to country.

Liquidity. Debt servicing difficulties of a country may result either from cyclical or accidental fluctuations in exports, from capital inflow and imports, or from a bunching of repayment obligations. It also may be a symptom of structural weaknesses in the economy. In other words, it can be a result of either purely transitory disturbances, long-term factors, or a combination of both.[19]

Liquidity indicators judge a country's ability to meet short-term obligations. From them, much insight can be obtained into the present foreign exchange condition of the country and its ability to remain solvent in the event of adversities. Essentially, these indicators are useful to compare short-term obligations with the short-term resources available to meet these obligations.

The debt service ratio, i.e., the ratio of debt service to exports, and the ratio of reserves to imports is the most frequently used indicator of liquidity. The debt service ratio has been used as a 'rule of thumb' in appraising the creditworthiness of borrowing countries. Similar to the 2-to-1 ratio currently accepted as the maximum financial ratio of a firm, 20 percent was widely believed to be the maximum acceptable level of the debt service ratio. Many financially sound countries have debt service ratios of less than 20 percent. At the same time, many countries with higher ratios have continuously borrowed and repaid without serious debt servicing difficulties. Thus this ratio should be used in relation to the other measurements, such as growth and debt structure. In addition, to be a relevant indicator of the liquidity position at the time when a borrowing country should repay its obligation, the ratio should be either an expected future debt service ratio (DSR_{t+n}) or an expected change in the debt service ratio ((DSR_{t+n}- DSR_{t-1}) $\div$ DSR_{t-1}), if one can evaluate properly the future ratio. The data on debt service in the near future based on debt disbursed and outstanding in period t have been readily available from the public sources. In this study, an expected change in the debt service ratio will be used. The lower the ratio, the higher will be the debt servicing capacity.

The ratio of reserves to imports provides a similar measure of liquidity, as does the debt service ratio. Like the acid-test ratio which considers only the highly liquid portion of current assets, the ratio of reserves to imports considers as a means of payment only reserves which include the official gold holdings, convertible foreign exchange, and the country's net position (the ceiling of permissible borrowings less the amount of borrowings already incurred) at the International Monetary Fund. Reserves serve as a buffer against foreign exchange earnings such as might be caused by a sharp drop in the prices of the borrower's exports or by a crop failure necessitating very large imports. While the opportunity cost of maintaining foreign exchange and gold reserves lets a country reduce its need to maintain large reserves, *ceteris paribus*, the higher the ratio of reserves to imports, the higher will be the ability to serve external debt obligations. Unlike the debt service ratio, an expected future ratio of reserves to imports can hardly be obtained, because there is no precise available method of predicting the change in reserves.

Debt structure. For the analysis of debt structure, the ratio of total outstanding debt to GDP or the ratio of total outstanding debt to exports can be used. These indicators reveal the long-term liquidity of a country. We cannot conclude that the high ratio of debt to GDP or to exports is always a serious indication of creditworthiness without analyzing the use of the funds borrowed externally. If the debt's contribution to the productivity of the economy as a whole is higher than its cost, the ratio of debt to GDP or to exports does not convey any significant meaning. However, comparing the magnitude of foreign debt for a given country with those of other countries will suggest a 'general' indication of its creditworthiness. For this study, the ratio of total outstanding debt to the export of goods and services will be used.

In their study based on reschedulings, Frank and Cline include the ratio of debt amortization to total outstanding debt to evaluate "short-run flexibility in reducing debt service commitments by the temporary reduction of borrowing."[20] They argued that the low value for this ratio suggests that a country has predominantly long-term debt liabilities. Thus the country is more likely to reschedule. This argument is implausible. On the contrary, a longer maturity of liabilities provides borrowing countries with more leeway to cope with coming debt service difficulties. This ratio is not included in this study because the test result is not anticipated to show positive results since the maturity of the loans supplied by the official lenders has been decided based on the country's debt servicing capacity, extending loan maturity longer to less credit-worthy countries.

Coverage ratio. Coverage ratios such as the interest coverage ratio or the cash flow (interest and principal) coverage ratio are used extensively in evaluating a company's creditworthiness by such bond-rating services as Moody's Investors Service and Standard & Poor's.[21] The ratio of debt service payments to net capital inflows is the counterpart in the analysis of preparing a profile on a country. The capital inflow to a country -- in the form of grants, loans, suppliers' credits, foreign direct investment, transfer payments -- depends upon the country's economic and political situations. For example, foreign direct investment tends to fluctuate in response to changing conditions in both the capital importing and exporting countries. Loans and grants provided by governments are influenced largely by political considerations. If capital inflow were sufficient to allow a country to meet its debt servicing obligations, even if capital inflow is determined by political and economic considerations, it is obvious that the country would have no debt servicing problem.[22] Thus, the lower the ratio of debt service payments to capital inflows, the higher will be its creditworthiness. In the test reported here, the net capital inflow is the net trade balance plus the net capital account balance before debt service.

Political stability. Political stability is the state of harmony in society which enables mutually accepted and regular processes of government between the government and the governed. It originates from the existence of consensus, which is "a tacit agreement, engendered by a homogeneous political culture between the government and the governed as well as among groups within the governed, concerning the broad goal of society within a given time context and the means to implement its attainment."[23] Thus in consensual society, every significant policy must be based on at least general acquiescence or grudging acceptance.

According to the definition of T. Tsurutani, consensus neither signifies unanimity, nor necessarily assumes a democratic republic. Consensus exists because the government does not pursue a goal that the governed are unwilling or cannot be induced to pursue:

> A monarchy may very well be consensual if there is this fundamental mutual harmony between the rule and the ruled. So can aristocratic policy be consensual. So-called authoritarian society can, for the same reason, be consensual if it enjoys general approval, tacit or otherwise, of the people at large. Popular participation as such in politics does not necessarily make for democracy, let alone consensus. Conversely, neither consensus nor democracy requires universal popular participation as the *sine qua non*.[24]

Attainment of the goal that the governed are willing to pursue always requires sacrifices of resources that could otherwise be consumed for immediate or short-run physical or psychological gratifications. Thus in the consensual society there is always a stable trade-off between the goal and the means to achieve the goal. If there is a phenomenon of imbalance between goal and means, frustration or tension between the government and the governed arises which in turn spells political insecurity.

This study measures this political stability, using an index of political instability (stability) which was developed based on the available scalogram analysis of political instability.[25] The operational definition of political instability is the irregular political actions which the law of the country does not forbid. These actions differ depending upon the political structure of the country. For example, a certain demonstration which is an irregular political action in one country may be allowed in other countries as a regular political action. Nonetheless the following actions are considered to be political irregularities representing political instability: demonstrations, strikes, riots, politically motivated assassinations, coups d'etat, revolts, guerrillas, civil wars and revolutions.[26]

In this study the measure of political instability developed by I. Feierabend and R. Feierabend (1969, 1973) is used, because the validity of scaling has been confirmed by Guttman scaling and consensual validation techniques which ask judges to sort the same events along the same continuum. In this measure the intensity of irregular events as well as the frequency of their occurrence are taken into account, because these irregular events have different impacts on political stability. Their measure is a seven-point scale of political stability, ranging from zero to six. Each point of the scale is observantly defined differing degrees of stability. The scale is as follows:

	scale position (weight)
general elections	0
dismissals or resignations of officeholders	1
strikes and demonstrations	2
riots and assassinations	3
large-scale arrests and imprisonments	4
revolts and coups d'etat	5
guerrilla and civil wars and revolutions	6

The highest numbered positions represent the more serious irregular events. Each event is defined in Appendix II.

Based on these scale positions, a three-digit political instability index score which ranges from 0 to 699 is calculated for each nation. The first digit represents the scale position attached to the most irregular event occurring within the country over the time period being considered. Thus the countries with the same most irregular event are assigned to the same first digit group. The remaining two digits represent the sum of the weights (up to 99) assigned to each of the irregular events occurring within the country over the time period. These digits determine a country's relative position within the first digit group. The last two digits are measured in the following way:

$$PI = X_{ij} \cdot W_j$$

where PI_i = index of political instability (stability) of a country;
X_i = number of irregular events of a country;
W = weights of the irregular events

The number of irregular political events will be the sum of the last five years.

Willingness to pay. To be creditworthy, it is necessary for a country to channel its foreign borrowings into profitable investments.

But the country also should have a capacity to reconcile the competing claims on total resources, savings, and foreign exchange resources. Otherwise, the country would allow the public and private consumption to rise at a rate that exceeds the growth of additional output.[27] Under what conditions, then, will a country be able to develop a margin for debt service substantial enough to fulfill debt servicing without interruptions? The country's political and economic structures and ability to enhance governmental efficiency in utilizing resources for natural goals are important factors in the answer. Specifically, a strong government supported by general consensus may be able to squeeze domestic consumptions more efficiently. A country which imports more compressible goods and services, such as the non-necessary consumption goods, may have leeway to cut imports in times of foreign exchange shortage without having a serious impact on the economy.[28] But willingness to pay will be ultimately determined by future borrowings. If a country continues to borrow externally, it cannot repudiate its previous borrowings, which will precipitate a sudden fall in the creditworthiness of the country. This will, in turn, greatly diminish the country's future access to private capital markets as well as to international financing organizations. Thus in this study the proxy for willingness to pay will be the future anticipated borrowings. Since we cannot exactly quantify the future borrowings, the country's borrowing trends will be used as proxy. The trend will be based on the percentage change over the last three years in borrowings from the private capital markets as well as the international financing organization.

It should be noted that most lending to LDCs is guaranteed, and the available compilation of data is limited to the external public and publicly guaranteed debt of LDCs. When lending to LDCs is guaranteed by residents of another country, the capacity of the borrower's debt servicing and willingness to pay may not be the important consideration, since the guarantor will assume the ultimate obligation of debt servicing should the borrower default or repudiate its loan. Consequently, the analysis of creditworthiness based on the debt of LDCs may not be relevant. But according to the results of a survey[29] of foreign lending by large United States banks as of June 30, 1977, by the office of the Comptroller of the Currency, the Federal Deposit Insurance Corporation, and the Federal Reserve Board, the difference in lending to LDCs between country of borrower and country of guarantor is insignificant as shown in Table 3-2.

Table 3-2

U.S. Banks' Cross-border and Non-local Currency Lending to Foreigners as of June 1977* (in millions of U.S. dollars)

Non-oil Exporting LDCs	Lending to LDCs (country of borrower)	Lending to LDCs (country of guarantor)
Latin America and Caribbean	28,652	27,959
Asia	9,615	9,675
Africa	1,881	1,672
	40,148	39,306

*Includes claims of a maturity of under one year, but excludes claims of the offshore banking centers of the Bahamas, Bahrain, Caymans, Hong Kong, Panama, Singapore, Liberia, and Lebanon.

Source: Federal Reserve Board, "Country Exposure Lending Survey," January 16, 1978, Table 2.

In summary, creditworthiness of LDCs can be measured in terms of growth, level of development, liquidity, debt structure, coverage ratio, political stability, and willingness to pay:

$$CW_i = f(GI_i, GE_i, I_i, DSR_i, RI_i, D_i, C_i, P_i, W_i) \qquad (7)$$

where,

CW = creditworthiness of an individual country proxied by loans supplied ÷ needs. The loan amounts supplied are the annual commitments by the private financial markets.

GI = average annual rate of growth in per capita income over the last four years

GE = average annual rate of growth in exports over the last four years

DSR = expected change in debt service ratio
$(DSR_{t+2} - DSR_{t-1}) \div (DSR_{t-1})$

RI = ratio of reserves to imports for the year t-1

D = total outstanding debt to exports for the year t-1

C = coverage ratio represented by the ratio of debt service payments to net capital inflow for the year t-1

P   =   political stability index proxied by the product of the
        number of occurrences of irregular political events
        and the weights thereon over the previous five years
        (Feierabend & Feierabend political instability index)

W   =   willingness to pay proxied by the percentage change
        in borrowings in the last three years from the private
        capital markets and the international organizations

Data

Most of the data such as GDP, population, and balance of
payments were obtained from the International Monetary Fund's
International Financial Statistics and the *Balance of Payments Yearbook*,
from the United Nations' *Statistical Yearbook*, and from the World
Bank's *World Table 1976*. Data for political stability were retrieved from
the *Cross-National Time-Series Data Archives* originally collected by
Arthur S. Banks.

Quantification of credit from the private capital markets presents
some problem. The availability and accuracy of data are limited. There
are five data sources: (1) The Bank of England; (2) Bank for
International Settlements; (3) Development Assistance Committee of the
OECD; (4) World Bank Capital Market System; and (5) World Bank
Debtor Reporting System (see Figure 3-1).[30]

Bank of England. Bank of England source is the funds flow
from the London eurocurrency market to each country. Such statistics
are collected by the Bank of England in "External liabilities and claims
of banks in the United Kingdom in overseas currencies." Since these
external liabilities and claims represent all transactions with banks in the
U.K., they do not exactly represent the Eurocredit itself. To make it
more difficult, the London market is only part of the total Euromarket; it
represents about 45 percent of the Bank for International Settlement
(BIS) Inner Reporting Area of eight European countries and around 32
percent of all offshore banking centers.

Bank for International Settlement. BIS compiles and publishes
annually in the BIS *Annual Report* the information on the Eurocurrency
and Eurobond markets based on the reports made by banks in the
member countries of the Group of Ten, and Switzerland, and branches
of the U.S. banks located in the Caribbean area and in the Far East. A
detailed breakdown of the reporting banks' assets and liabilities *vis-a-vis*
many individual LDCs is published quarterly. The BIS statistics include
all short-term loans and unpublicized Eurocredits to private borrowers,
which are not recorded in other data sources. But this information

includes neither gross new lending for a given period, amortization, and interest payments, nor Eurocurrency credits and loans by banks not in Group of Ten countries and Switzerland.

Development Assistance Committee (Expanded Reporting System). This statistical system is based on reports made annually by the DAC member countries on the amount, terms, nature, and geographical distribution of these flows of resources from both official and private sources. Information compiled through this system is published annually in the report of the Chairman of the DAC, *Developing Cooperation: Efforts and Policies of the Members of Development Assistance Committee.* Only flows to developing countries and multilateral institutions are included. Flows to developing countries from countries not members of the DAC are excluded, as are most Eurocurrency transactions and short-term loans.

Capital Market System. This information is based on published reports collected by the World Bank. It includes publicized Eurocurrency credits and foreign and international bond issues. This information has been prepared since 1973 and circulated since the third quarter of 1974 in the quarterly report, *Borrowing in International Capital Markets.* The report includes individual lending commitment, but does not include drawings and repayment. While these data are more comprehensive and specific than other information on publicized credits, there are many occasions when loans for substantial amounts have not been publicized for undisclosed reasons. This makes it difficult to estimate the correct amount of borrowing of LDCs.

Debtor Reporting System. This information is the World Bank's *World Debt Tables* compiled by reports from developing countries which have received either IBRD loans or IDA credits. The data are cross-checked by the World Bank with data from several other sources, i.e., the Expanded Reporting System from the members of DAC of the OECD and statistics in the *Borrowing in International Capital Markets.* These *World Debt Tables'* data contain information on the external debt of the 84 LDCs by country and type of creditor. The creditors are categorized as loans from governments, loans from international organizations, suppliers' credits, credits from private financial markets, and other obligations to private lenders. The report includes commitments, withdrawals, amortization and debt service. Because credits from private banks and bonds are included under the same heading of 'credits from financial markets,' it is impossible to identify the exact amount of credits from private banks. Relying on these data is the better alternative under the circumstances, however, because the issuances of bonds by LDCs are insignificant compared to total credits from private banks and other private financial institutions (slightly less than ten percent of total credits from private sources). In addition, these data are the most comprehensive and cover the periods of this study.

Figure 3-2. Schematic Information on Financial Flows to LDCs
Source: IMF, *IMF Survey*, September 6, 1976, pp. 264-265.

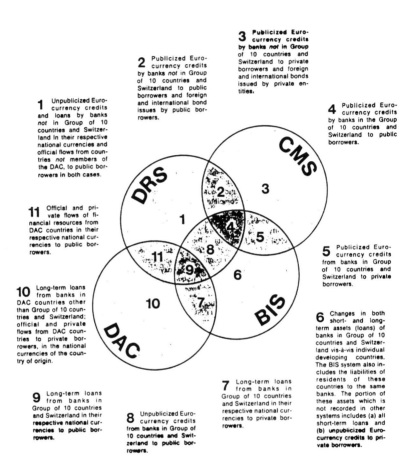

1 Unpublicized Euro-currency credits and loans by banks *not* in Group of 10 countries and Switzerland in their respective national currencies and official flows from countries *not* members of the DAC, to public borrowers in both cases.

2 Publicized Euro-currency credits by banks *not* in Group of 10 countries and Switzerland to public borrowers and foreign and international bond issues by public borrowers.

3 Publicized Euro-currency credits by banks *not* in Group of 10 countries and Switzerland to private borrowers and foreign and international bonds issued by private entities.

4 Publicized Euro-currency credits by banks in the Group of 10 countries and Switzerland to public borrowers.

5 Publicized Euro-currency credits from banks in Group of 10 countries and Switzerland to private borrowers.

6 Changes in both short- and long-term assets (loans) of banks in Group of 10 countries and Switzerland vis-à-vis individual developing countries. The BIS system also includes the liabilities of residents of these countries to the same banks. The portion of these assets which is not recorded in other systems includes (a) all short-term loans and (b) unpublicized Euro-currency credits to private borrowers.

7 Long-term loans from banks in Group of 10 countries and Switzerland in their respective national currencies to private borrowers.

8 Unpublicized Euro-currency credits from banks in Group of 10 countries and Switzerland to public borrowers.

9 Long-term loans from banks in Group of 10 countries and Switzerland in their respective national currencies to public borrowers.

10 Long-term loans from banks in DAC countries other than Group of 10 countries and Switzerland; official and private flows from DAC countries to private borrowers, in the national currencies of the country of origin.

11 Official and private flows of financial resources from DAC countries in their respective national currencies to public borrowers.

NOTES

[1]Among the published information on debt reschedulings are: World Bank Group, *Multinational Debt Renegotiations since 1956*, May 1973; Henry J. Bittermann, *The Refunding of International Debt*, 1973; and Robert N. Bee, "Lesson from Debt Reschedulings in the Past," *Euromoney*, April 1977.

[2]Steven I. Davis, *The Euro-Bank: Its Origins, Managements, and Outlook* (New York: John Wiley & Sons, 1976), p. 98.

[3]Simon S. Kuznets, *Modern Economic Growth: Rate, Structure, and Spread* (New Haven: Yale University Press, 1966).

[4]E.S. Mason defines the absorptive capacity as that volume of investment at which the marginal rate of return is equal to the "socially acceptable discount rate."   See E.S. Mason, *On the Appropriate Size of a Development Program*, Occasional Papers in International Affairs, No. 8, Cambridge, Mass., August 1964.

[5]The concept of 'need' in this model is similar to the 'need' for foreign resource transfers (international aid) within the framework of the growth catalyst theory.   The 'need' for external financial requirements is equal to the gap between the desirable level of investment and self-generated savings, or the gap between imports required to secure the target growth rate and the country's export earnings.   See Ravi L. Gulhati, "The 'Need' for Foreign Resources, Absorptive Capacity and Debt Servicing Capacity," in *Capital Movements and Economic Development*, edited by J. Adler and P. Kuznets (New York: St. Martin's Press, 1967), p. 245.

[6]In the Harrod-Domar model, the rate of growth is the product of the savings rate and of the capital-output ratio.   Under the assumption that there is no substitutability between capital and labor, and that labor is in surplus supply, capital becomes the overriding constraint for the economic developments of LDCs.   The Harrod-Domar model is modified later by R. Solow (1956) and J. Meade (1963), who provided for substitution among factors, rather than the fixed proportions assumed by the original model, and by N. Kaldor (1957) who explained it using a technical-progress function related to investment.

[7]See E.K. Hawkins, "Measuring Capital Requirments," *Development and Finance*, June 1968, pp. 2-7.

[8]Everett E. Hagen, *The Economics of Development* (revised edition; Homewood, Ill.: Richard D. Irwin, 1975), p. 350.

[9]E.K. Hawkins, op. cit., p. 6.

[10]In this study, the average incremental capital-output ratio for the study period will be used.

[11]A low ratio is desirable over a long period of time insofar as it applies to the entire economy.   With regard to a particular project or sector, the ratio depends upon many factors and nothing can be said about its being good or bad.   For example, most LDCs prefer labor-intensive industry rather than capital-intensive industry to absorb their abundant labor forces.

[12]G. Alter asserts that the target growth rate of per capita income, compared with the rate that can be achieved in the absence of foreign capital inflow, may be put at a higher level, and a larger volume of foreign capital inflow is permitted when:

    (1) the marginal savings ratio is higher;

    (2) the incremental capital-output ratio is lower;

    (3) the rate of population increase is lower;

    (4) the required rate of return on foreign capital inflow is lower;

    (5) the degree of independence of foreign capital that must be achieved within a given time period is lower;

    (6) the time period in which a given degree of independence must be achieved is longer.

See Gerald M. Alter, "The Servicing of Foreign Capital Inflows by Under-developed Countries," in *Economic Development of Latin America*, edited by Howard S. Ellis. New York: St. Martin's Press, 1962, p. 149.

[13]Dragoslav Avramovic, et al., *Economic Growth and External Debt* (Baltimore, Md.: Johns Hopkins Press, 1964), p. 7.

[14]Raymond F. Mikesell, "The Capacity to Service Foreign Investment," in *U.S. Private and Government Investment Abroad*, edited by R.F. Mikesell (Eugene: University of Oregon, 1962), p. 378.

[15]Gunter Dufey and Sangkee Min, *The Access of Developing Countries to International Credit*, Working Paper #148, Graduate School of Business Administration, The University of Michigan, p. 24.

[16]Raymond F. Mikesell, *Public International Lending for Development* (New York: Random House, Inc., 1966), p. 183.

[17]Gerald M. Alter, op. cit., p. 140.

[18]In 1971 the United Nations Committee for Development Planning identified a group of countries to be termed the "least developed," based on three criteria: (1) GDP of $100 or less (in 1968), (2) a share of manufacturing in GDP of 10% or less, and (3) a literacy rate of 20% or less within the population 15 years of age and over (around 1960).

[19]D. Avramovic, et al., op. cit., p. 11.

[20]Charles R. Frank and William R. Cline, "Measurement of Debt Servicing Capacity: An Application of Discriminant Analysis," p. 332.

[21]James C. Van Horne, *Financial Management and Policy* (4th ed.; Englewood Cliffs, N.J.: Prentice-Hall, 1977), p. 682.

[22]D. Avramovic, et al., op. cit., p. 21.

[23]Taketsugu Tsurutani, "Stability and Instability: A Note in Comparative Political Analysis," *The Journal of Politics*, November 1968, p. 911. Definitions of political stability differ depending upon the field of comparative political analysis. The common denominator of the definition, however, is the 'consensus' among the members of

society. For example, C. Ake defines political stability as the "regularity of the flow of political exchanges. The more regular the flow of political exchanges, the more stability. Alternatively, we might say that there is political stability to the extent that members of society restrict themselves to the behavior patterns that fall within the limits imposed by political role expectations. Any act that deviates from these limits is an instance of political instability." See Claude Ake, "A Definition of Political Stability," *Comparative Politics*, January 1975, pp. 271-283.

[24]T. Tsurutani, op. cit., p. 912.

[25]There are many ways to ascertain the political stability of a country through the use of cross-national data. Among them, two methods are most frequently used: factor analysis and scalogram analysis. The factor analysis involves "the identification of several dimensions (factors) of conflict behavior -- that is, clusters of violent events that frequently occur together but are unrelated to such clusters." Scalogram analysis develops "several scaling instruments of irregular political events ranging from simple consensual and construct-validity scales to more complicated ones, such as the Guttman scalogram." See Ivo K. Feierabend, et al., "The Comparative Study of Revolution Violence," *Comparative Politics*, pp. 393-424.

[26]See Betty A. Nesvold, "Scalogram Analysis of Political Violence," *Comparative Political Studies*, July 1969, pp. 172-194, and I. Feierabend, et al., op. cit., p. 396. B. Nesvold (1969) used a four position scale and L. Feierabend, et al. (1973) used a seven position scale. Despite the difference in total number of scale positions, the pattern of scaling in both cases is similar except for riots. Nesvold also was a participant in the study by Feierabend.

[27]G. Dufey and S. Min, op. cit., p. 24.

[28]One common quantitative measure of willingness of a municipal unit to pay its debt obligations (in measuring municipal bond quality) is the relationship between before-tax personal income and taxes. A lower ratio of tax to personal income indicates the municipal unit has more leeway to cut private consumptions in times of adversity so that the municipal unit with a lower ratio is more creditworthy. G. Hempel argues that "A good tax collection, especially in periods of adversity, indicates to some extent the willingness of residents to meet their tax liabilities." See George H. Hempel, *Measures of Municipal Bond Quality*, Bureau of Business Research, Graduate School of Business Administration, The University of Michigan, 1967, pp. 33-34.

[29]Federal Reserve Board, "Country Exposure Lending Survey," January 16, 1978. The bank regulatory agencies have instituted a semi-annual "Country Exposure Report" to begin with data for December 1977. The data cover claims on foreign residents held at all domestic and foreign offices of 119 U.S. banks with assets of $1 billion or more.

[30]For detailed information, see IMF, *IMF Survey*, September 6, 1976 and the World Bank, *Borrowing in International Capital Markets*, EC-181 Supplement, August 1976.

CHAPTER IV

EMPIRICAL EVIDENCE

The function hypothesized in equation (7) was tested by cross-section regression analysis on the data of the 33 LDCs which had borrowed from commercial financing sources during the period 1971-1975. The countries included most of the LDCs listed in the *World Debt Tables: External Public Debt of Developing Countries.* For these countries, total debt outstanding from private financial markets was $26.5 billion as of 1975, or 72.6 percent of LDC's total financing. The test excluded: (a) the oil exporting countries such as Iran, Iraq, Venezuela, Ecuador, Indonesia, Syria, Trinidad and Tobago; (b) small and/or recently independent countries such as Benin, Botswana, Burundi, Cameron, and Chad; and, (c) communist countries such as Yugoslavia and the People's Republic of Congo.[1]

Creditworthiness Index (Dependent Variable)

The dependent variable in the regression was the creditworthiness index developed from the Harrod-Domar model, as explained in the previous chapter. The index was the product of the loan amounts supplied from the commercial financing sources, divided by the external financing requirements. Its value ranged between one and zero:

$$\text{Creditworthiness Index} = \frac{Q}{\text{need}} = \frac{Q}{\text{GDP}(g^* \cdot \text{ICOR} - s - p)}$$

where Q = loan amounts supplied from the commercial financing sources;

g^* = target income growth rate;

ICOR = incremental capital-output ratio;

s = national savings rate;

p = ratio of total amounts financing from the public sources to GDP.

As discussed in the previous chapter, the index values changed depending upon target income growth rate, g^*, so selection of the applicable target rate was important. Using heuristic procedures, we determined the target growth rate to be 18 percent. When the target growth rate of 16 percent was applied, some of the index values were negative; when the target growth rate of 17 percent was applied, the maximum index value was 1.296, which was beyond the hypothesized maximum index value, 1.0 (see Table 4-1). Thus any target growth rate above 18 percent could be applied for the creditworthiness index.

Table 4-1

Descriptive Measure of Creditworthiness Index
with Various Target Growth Rates

Target Growth Rate (percentage)	Index Values			
	Minimum	Maximum	Mean	Std. Dev.
21	.0003	.2017	.0377	.0426
20	.0003	.2197	.0415	.0477
19	.0004	.2514	.0465	.0553
18	.0004	.4146	.0537	.0696
17	.0004	1.2955	.0705	.1365
16	-1.1515	2.1903	.0712	.2418

For this study, the index based on 18 percent growth rate was chosen. (The stability of the model depending upon the index values will be mentioned later in this chapter.) Because the index values vary according to the target growth rate applied, importance should be given to the relative value, rather than the absolute value of the indices.

Frequency distribution of countries in terms of their degree of relative creditworthiness is presented in Figure 4-1. The distribution is skewed. Lower index values are more prevalent than higher ones within the sample of countries, and the majority of countries are classified under the low creditworthiness indices. The distribution is not suprising since most LDCs probably have limited access to the private financing sources; thus, the numerator of the index (the amounts supplied) would be very low compared to the denominator (the financing requirements).

Determinants of Creditworthiness

It was hypothesized that the creditworthiness of a country is a function of (1) growth in income (GI), (2) level of development (I), (3) liquidity (DSR and RI), (4) debt structure (D), (5) coverage ratio (C), (6) willingness to pay (W), and (7) political stability (P). The explanatory variables for this function were discussed in detail in Chapter III.

	Philippines				
	Morocco				
Turkey	El Salvador				
Pakistan	Paraguay				
Thailand	Argentina				
Sierra Leone	Uruguay				
Kenya	Egypt				
Malawi	Jamaica	Ivory Coast			
Chile	Colombia	Mexico			
Honduras	Sudan	Costa Rica	Dominican		
India	Guyana	Zaire	Malaysia	Brazil	
Sri Lanka	Guatemala	Greece	Korea	Peru	Taiwan

| 0 | .04 | .08 | .12 | .16 | .20 |

Less creditworthy – – – – – – – – – – – – – – – – – – More creditworthy

Min = .001 Max = .196   Mean = .054 Std. Dev. = .053

Figure 4-1

Frequency Distribution of Countries in Terms of Their Degree of Relative Creditworthiness, 1971-1975
(For the exact index value of each country, see Appendix III.)

Since 1973 was the latest year for which data on the political stability variable was available, two stages of analysis were performed: (1) estimation without the political stability variable for the period 1971-1975; (2) estimation with the political stability variable for the period 1971-1974.

Estimation Without the Political Stability Variable. Least square multiple regressions of the equation without the political stability variable were performed on yearly data for the period 1971-1975. Yearly data were used because (based on the country exposure reporting procedures) although the majority of commercial banks set country exposure limits on a quarterly basis,[2] consistent available data for analysis are available on a yearly basis. In addition, the loan amounts used in the creditworthiness index are yearly commitments by the private financial markets.

The regression yielded the following results:

CW =   -2.989 + 0.237 GI + 0.017 GE + 0.00001 I - 2.991 DSR
        (-2.181)   (8.187)*   (2.218)*   (0.775)   (-2.170)*

-0.035 RI - 0.00001 D - 0.0004 C + 0.0001 W
(-1.289)   (-2.149)*   (-0.788)   (1.196)

R^2 = 0.487,   S.E.E. = 0.051.   (8)

The values of the t-statistics are shown in parentheses. Those marked with an asterisk (*) are statistically significant at the .05 level. All coefficients in the multiple regressions were congruent with the theoretically expected signs except the sign of the reserves/imports ratio which was negatively related to the creditworthiness index and was statistically insignificant.

There were some complications of multicollinearity among explanatory variables. As Figure 4-2 shows, the correlation between growth in GDP and growth in exports especially was statistically significant. To remove the multicollinearity between these two variables, the export growth variable was dropped from the equation. Dropping the export growth variable from the model did not jeopardize the integrity of the model, because the growth in the GDP variable alone was representative of most of the "*growth*." Even after dropping the export growth variable, some multicollinearity remained between the debt/exports ratio and the debt service ratio, and between the per capita income and the debt service ratio at the .01 level, but these were not significant enough to necessitate changing the hypothesized model in order to correct multicollinearity (see Figure 4-3).

Estimation without the export growth variable yielded the following results:

CW =   -2.861 + 0.267 GI + 0.00001 I - 2.867 DSR - 0.031 RI - 0.00001 D
        (-2.064) (10.284)*   (1.299)   (-2.056)*   (-1.143)   (-2.350)*

-0.004 C + 0.00007 W
(-0.811)   (0.928)   (9)

R^2 = 0.471   S.E.E. = 0.052

*statistically significant at the .05 level

Table 4-2
Summary of Regressions Using Different Target Growth Rates for Creditworthiness Index (for the Period 1971-1975)

Creditworthiness as function of variable	21%		20%		19%		18%	
	Coefficient	t-statistics	Coefficient	t-statistics	Coefficient	t-statistics	Coefficient	t-statistics
Constant	-1.978	-2.151*	-2.168	-2.154*	-2.429	-2.156*	-2.861	-2.064*
GI	0.135	7.832*	0.160	8.499*	0.199	9.375*	0.287	10.284*
I	0.00001	1.714*	0.00001	1.660*	0.0001	1.557	0.00001	1.299
DSR	-1.994	-2.157*	-2.184	-2.156*	-2.442	-2.145*	-2.867	-2.056*
RI	-0.021	-1.181	-0.024	-1.199	0.027	-1.208	-0.031	-1.143
D	-0.00001	-2.744*	-0.00001	-2.683*	-0.0001	-2.579*	-0.0001	-2.350*
C	-0.0003	-0.759	-0.0003	-0.779	-0.0004	-0.803	-0.0004	-0.811
W	0.00007	1.336	0.0007	1.279	0.00008	1.173	0.00007	0.928
S.E.E.	0.034		0.038		0.042		0.052	
R^2	0.380		0.407		0.441		0.471	

*Statistically significant at the .10 level

	GI	GE	RI	DSR	W	D	I	C
GI	1.000							
GE	.485	1.000						
RI	.199	.168	1.000					
DSR	-.085	-.042	-.173	1.000				
W	.001	-.125	-.083	-.005	1.000			
D	-.177	-.207	.015	-.023	-.013	1.000		
I	.032	.245	.116	-.252	-.109	-.152	1.000	
C	.030	.001	-.032	-.005	-.003	-.052	-.025	1.000
	GI	GE	RI	DSR	W	D	I	C

*Significant at the level, .05 = .153   .01 = .200

Figure 4-2

Correlation Matrix of Independent Variables

	GI	RI	DSR	W	D	I	C
GI	1.000						
RI	.199	1.000					
DSR	-.085	-.173	1.000				
W	.001	-.083	-.005	1.000			
D	-.177	.015	-.234	-.013	1.000		
I	.032	.116	-.252	-.109	-.152	1.000	
C	.030	-.032	-.005	-.033	-.052	-.025	1.000
	GI	RI	DSR	W	D	I	C

*Significant at the level, .05 = .153   .01 = .200

Figure 4-3

Correlation Matrix of Independent Variables Without Export
Growth Variable

The signs of all coefficients except the reserves/imports ratio
were as expected. The sign of coefficient of the reserves/imports ratio
was negatively related with the creditworthiness index, while the ratio

was not statistically significant even at .2 level. The estimates of the coefficients were significant at the .05 level for three variables: GDP growth, change in debt service ratio, and debt/exports ratio. The coefficient of determination, R^2, was good for a cross-section regression of this size which did not have any trend variables; diagnostic checking did not reveal any systematic pattern underlying the generated residuals.

The average growth rate of real GDP and per capita income were positively related to the creditworthiness index. The growth of real GDP was absolutely significant at all levels, while the per capita income was statistically significant only at the .20 level. This confirms that the present stage of economic development is an important short term consideration in determining the creditworthiness of a country, but for the long run, the growth of GDP is the only important factor in the creditworthiness of a country.

Both liquidity ratios, the debt service ratio and the reserves/imports ratio in the previous year were not statistically significant, suggesting that such single point indicators of a country's liquidity position were not as important as changing trends over a period of time. In fact, contrary to the theoretical argument, the debt service ratio in the year t-1 was positively related to the creditworthiness index, and the reserves/imports ratio was negatively related. This outcome of the debt service ratio can be explained, however, because the country with greater creditworthiness could borrow a relatively higher amount of external debt so that the debt service requirements in the following years could become higher compared to the export income.

The change in the expected debt service ratio (DSR_{t+2} - DSR_{t-1}) ÷ (DSR_{t-1}) was defined as an expected change in the debt service ratio between periods t-1 and t+2. The data on debt service in period t+2 were readily available from the *World Bank's World Debt Tables* and were based on debt disbursed and outstanding in period t. The average annual rate of growth of exports during the three years prior to t was used to project exports in periods t+1 and t+2. The coefficient for the change in expected debt service ratio was negatively related to the creditworthiness index, indicating that the absolute level of the debt service ratio at any point in time was important largely in relation to possible future changes in that ratio. The result of the reserves/imports ratio was surprising because the sign of its coefficient was not as expected, even though the coefficient was not statistically significant.[3] This result has two possible explanations: bankers who made decisions on country exposure limits did not care about the reserves/imports ratio, or the analysis might have some sort of statistical problem. The latter explanation is less likely because, as shown in Figure 4-2, there was no significant multicollinearity between the reserves/imports ratio and other explanatory variables, and the specification of the variable itself followed those used by practitioners and academicians.

The coefficient of the debt/exports ratio was negatively related to the creditworthiness and was significant at the .05 level. When the debt/GDP ratio was applied in the regression instead of the debt/exports ratio, it was positively related to the creditworthiness index. The creditworthy countries would have greater access to the external capital markets so that their debt/GDP ratios would become higher than those of less creditworthy countries. This result confirms that the high ratio of debt/GDP is not always a serious indication of creditworthiness without analyzing the use of the funds borrowed externally. In addition, for the analysis of debt structure or long-term liquidity, debt/exports is a more relevant indicator than debt/GDP ratio.

Although the coverage ratio was, as expected, negatively related to the creditworthiness index, it was not statistically significant. This may indicate that the coverage ratio for balance-of-payments has little meaning because, unlike the profit in the company, the net value added in the economy is not reflected in the balance-of-payments. In addition, any countries wanting to develop beyond their domestic resources, should import more goods and services, but this deficit in trade would be neutralized by a surplus in one of the capital accounts.

The willingness-to-pay variable was positively related to the creditworthiness index, but it was statistically significant only at the .25 level. It was proxied by the percentage change over the last three years in borrowings from the private capital markets as well as the international financing organizations. An alternative measure of willingness to pay was the ratio of the government revenue to GDP. It was negatively related to the creditworthiness index, and was statistically significant at the .05 level. It also suggests that countries with lower ratios have more leeway to cut private consumption in times of foreign exchange shortage in order to appear more creditworthy.[4]

To compare the difference in the contributions of respective variables in explaining creditworthiness, a stepwise (forward) regression was run. The results of the stepwise regression of analysis of creditworthiness at the .20 level for the inclusion and deletion of the variables is shown in Appendix IV. GDP growth was included in the first step. GDP growth alone explained 42 percent of the variations in creditworthiness. Debt/exports, change in debt service ratio, the ratio of government revenue to GDP, and per capita income were added but were not very significant in improving R^2. In other words, at the .20 level all the variables for growth, debt structure, liquidity, willingness to pay, and level of development (except for coverage) were statistically significant, but not as important as the variables for growth.

Estimation with political stability variable. Least square multiple regressions of equation (7) including the political stability variable was performed on yearly data for the period 1971-1974. The political stability variable was adopted from the available scalogram index of political instability developed by I. Feierabend and R. Feierabend (1969, 1973).

The average political stability indices of the 33 countries included in this study are shown in Figure 4-4. About half of the countries fell into the least stable position. (The 6 position included at least one incidence of guerrilla or civil war.)[5] The regression yielded the following results:

$$CW = \begin{array}{ccccc} -3.368 & + & 0.297 \ GI & + & 0.00002 \ I & - & 3.375 \ DSR & - & 0.387 \ RI \\ (-1.962) & & (10.535)^* & & (1.498) & & (-1.953)^* & & (-1.289) \end{array}$$

$$\begin{array}{cccc} -0.00001 \ D & - & 0.0002 \ C & + & 0.00007 \ W & - & 0.002 \ P \\ (-1.828) & & (-1.284) & & (0.934) & & (0.871) \end{array}$$

$$R^2 = 0.528 \qquad S.E.E. = 0.052 \qquad\qquad (12)$$

*Significant at the .05 level

The signs of all coefficients except the reserves/imports ratio in multiple regression were as theoretically expected.[6] The coefficient for political instability was negatively related to creditworthiness as expected. The higher the political instability index, the lower the creditworthiness. However, the introduction of the political instability variable improved the R^2 to only a very limited extent.[7] The coefficient was statistically insignificant at the .20 level. In addition, the size of the coefficient did not indicate any strong relationship between the creditworthiness of a country and its political stability.

The result can be interpreted so that the assessment of a country's political stability is important for creditworthiness to the extent of our *a priori* knowledge that bankers assign considerable weight to what they consider to be a politically stable government, but only as a subjective evaluation. If one could make the quantitative assessment, any quantification similar to the Feierabend and Feierabend method used for this study could not be the sole measure for assessing political stability, because any one measure of political stability could hardly capture the complex web of political relationships.

		Ivory Coast		Argentina Philippines Chile Brazil Sudan Pakistan Guatemala Uruguay Greece Dominican Malaysia Thailand
Costa Rica		Taiwan	Mexico	Colombia
El Salvador	Kenya	Egypt	Sri Lanka	Turkey
Jamaica	Peru	Morocco	Honduras	Korea
Malawi	Guyana	Paraguay	Sierra Leone	Zaire
1	2	3	4	5	6

Min = 50.5   Max = 699   Mean = 515   Std. Dev. = 191

Figure 4-4

**Frequency Distribution of Countries by Relative
Political Stability, 1968-1973**

Stability of Model

Stability of the model was determined through three different exercises: (1) a test of stability of the creditworthiness index, (2) a test using yearly data, and (3) a test using average values of yearly data.

As mentioned before, the index value of creditworthiness in the model changes depending upon the target growth rate, g^*. The higher the target growth rates, the lower the values of indices for the countries which borrowed less from the private capital markets. If the estimation results differ depending upon the different target rates, the use of the model using this creditworthiness index will be limited. Thus we should test the stability of the model for the different target growth rates.

Four different index values based on different target growth rates were taken as dependent variables in the regressions. The results of these regressions are summarized in Tables 4-2 and 4-3. Although there were some variations, the result of any one regression was not substantially different from those of other regressions. All the signs of the coefficients were the same; the statistical significance of coefficients changed to the limited extent; the R^2's decreased somewhat as the target growth rates increased, but not extremely. For example, the R^2 decreased from 0.471 in the estimation using an 18 percent target growth rate to 0.380 of the estimation using a 21 percent target growth rate for 1971-1975 data without political stability data. For 1971-1975 data with political stability data, R^2 decreased from 0.528 to 0.429. One possible explanation of the R^2 variations is that the data are somewhat heteroscedastic, almost all the indices have variances that increase with values.

The second exercise regressed the model to the yearly data from 1971 to 1975. Results of these regressions are shown in Tables 4-4 and 4-5. While there were some variations in R^2's and the significance of the coefficients, the results were basically the same.

The third exercise regressed the model to the average values of yearly data to remove possible serial correlations. Any data including time series observations may have some serial correlation among the regression residuals. The data for this study were partially in time series with five-year observations of 33 countries. But since all the variables in the model were either ratios or per capita data, the trend influence would be eliminated.[8] For the pooling of cross-sectional and time series data, there is no available method (like the Durbin-Watson test) to measure the existence of serial correlations in the unexplained variations from an equation fitted by the least-square method. Thus, to determine the absence of trend influence, one-time horizon (1975-1971) observations of each country were regressed. The one-time horizon observations obtained were to be average values for the five-year period; e.g.,

$$D = \frac{\text{Debt Outstanding 1974-1970}}{\text{Exports 1974-1970.}}$$

The results are as follows:

(For the period 1971-1975 without the political stability variable)

$$CW = \begin{array}{cccccc} -1.676 & + & 0.218 \ GI & + & 0.00002 \ I & - & 1.657 \ DSR & - & 0.063 \ RI \\ (-0.882) & & (5.042)* & & (1.266) & & (-0.864) & & (-1.390) \end{array}$$

$$\begin{array}{cccc} - & 0.000001 \ D & - & 0.0021 \ C & + & 0.016 \ W \\ & (-0.057) & & (-0.372) & & (3.065)* \end{array} \qquad (15)$$

$$R^2 = .654 \qquad S.E.E = 0.0297$$

*Significant at the .05 level

(For the period 1971-1974 with the political stability variable)

$$CW = \begin{array}{l} -3.418 \\ (-1.159) \end{array} + \begin{array}{l} 0.265 \\ (5.586)^* \end{array} GI + \begin{array}{l} 0.00001 \\ (0.720) \end{array} I - \begin{array}{l} 3.417 \\ (-1.149) \end{array} DSR - \begin{array}{l} 0.071 \\ (-1.531) \end{array} RI$$

$$\begin{array}{l} -0.0000002 \\ (-0.023) \end{array} D - \begin{array}{l} 0.0049 \\ (-0.771) \end{array} C + \begin{array}{l} 0.010 \\ (2.306)^* \end{array} W - \begin{array}{l} 0.000018 \\ (-0.437) \end{array} \qquad (16)$$

$$R^2 = 0.667 \qquad S.E.E. = 0.0356$$

Compared to the estimation (8) the results were not significantly different. In the estimation (8) three variables, GDP growth, change in debt service ratio, and debt/export, were significant at the 0.05 level, but two variables, GDP growth and willingness to pay, were significant while the signs of all coefficients remained the same. The R^2's have improved because of the reduction in yearly variations of the residuals.

From the above three exercises, we can assume that the model used in this study is stable within the appropriate target growth rates, and there is no significant variation in estimations on year-by-year data.

Relationships with Other Models Using Different Creditworthiness Indices

Aside from the creditworthiness index developed from the Harrod-Domar model, the indices using GDP or population as a proxy for external financing requirements such as loan supplied/GDP or loan supplied/population have been suggested. As mentioned in the previous chapter, these two indices have limitations because of the assumption that countries of the same economic size or the same population will need the same level of funding from the external financing. The indices do not reflect the savings potential, the productivity of capital, or the availability of other financing sources for the particular country.

An empirical comparison was made between the results of regressions using three indices with those of equation (7) in Tables 4-6 and 4-7. Compared to the regression results using the creditworthiness index based on the Harrod-Domar model [equation (7)] regression results using the indices of loan supplied/GDP and loan supplied/population neither exhibited much explanatory power as evidenced by small R^2's, nor showed the theoretically expected signs of the coefficients.

In the regression using the index of loan/GDP for the period 1971-1975, the growth of GDP was negatively related with the creditworthiness, the opposite of our expectations, and R^2 was only 0.103. In the regression using the index loan/population, the reserves/imports ratio was positively related as theoretically expected (as opposed to the index based on the Harrod-Domar model), but GDP growth was negatively related with the creditworthiness, and R^2 was 0.379, which is smaller by 0.087 than the result obtained using the index based on the Harrod-Domar model.   GDP growth was hypothesized as the most important explanatory variable.

To compare the fitness in terms of the standard error of estimation (S.E.E.), each of the three indices was divided by its geometric mean and regressed with the explanatory variables.[9]   The S.E.E. of each model was as follows:

S.E.E. of loan/GDP = 3.872 (R^2 = 0.013)
S.E.E. of loan/population = 14.862 (R^2 = 0.379)
S.E.E. of index of the Harrod-Domar Model = 3.359
        (R^2 = 0.471)

The regression using the index of the Harrod-Domar model had the lowest S.E.E. and could be considered best fitted in terms of S.E.E. Based on these two exercises it could be concluded that the model used in this study is a better one.

Table 4-3

Summary of Regressions Using Different Target Growth Rates for Creditworthiness Index (for the period 1971-1974 with political stability variable)

Creditworthiness as function of variable	21%		20%		19%		18%	
	Coefficient	t-statistics	Coefficient	t-statistics	Coefficient	t-statistics	Coefficient	t-statistics
Constant	-2.059	-1.846*	-2.295	-1.876*	-2.657	-1.927*	-3.368	-1.962*
GI	0.148	8.065*	0.176	8.771*	0.219	9.686*	0.297	10.535*
I	0.00001	1.888*	0.00001	1.853*	0.00001	1.765*	0.00002	1.498
DSR	-2.076	-1.848*	-2.311	-1.877*	-2.670	-1.923*	-3.375	-1.953*
RI	-0.280	-1.437	-0.309	-1.445	-0.346	-1.435	-0.387	-1.289
D	-0.00001	-2.207*	-0.00001	-2.148*	-0.00001	-2.048*	-0.00001	-1.828*
C	-0.00006	-0.125	-0.00008	-0.148	-0.00011	-0.193	-0.00021	-0.284
W	0.00007	1.361	0.00008	1.305	0.00008	1.197	0.00007	0.934
P	-0.00001	-0.658	-0.00001	-0.676	-0.00001	-0.731	-0.00002	-0.871
S.E.	0.034		0.037		0.042		0.052	
R^2	0.429		0.461		0.498		0.528	

*Statistically significant at the .10 level

Table 4-4

Summary of Regressions for Various Years (without Political Stability Variable)

Creditworthiness as function of variable	1971		1972		1973	
	Coefficient	t-statistics	Coefficient	t-statistics	Coefficient	t-statistics
Constant	-0.075	-0.266	-2.765	-1.213	-3.368	-0.679
GI	0.311	6.127*	0.266	7.787*	0.416	4.333*
I	0.00003	1.355	0.00003	1.293	0.00001	0.197
DSR	-0.044	-0.015	-2.765	-1.208	-3.340	-0.669
RI	-0.077	-1.348	-0.045	-0.837	-0.054	-0.669
D	-0.00001	-0.919	-0.00001	-1.463	-0.00001	-0.250
C	-0.005	-0.620	0.007	0.858	-0.002	-0.257
W	0.001	1.410	0.0006	0.068	0.002	0.651
S.E.E.	0.038		0.043		0.073	
R^2	0.663		0.755		0.474	

*Statistically significant at the .10 level.

Table 4-4 (Continued)

Creditworthiness as function of variable	1974		1975	
	Coefficient	t-statistics	Coefficient	t-statistics
Constant	-7.768	-1.942*	-5.499	-2.199*
GI	0.396	3.886*	0.081	1.308*
I	-0.00001	-0.350	-0.00001	-0.156
DSR	-7.795	-1.942*	-5.538	-2.198*
RI	-0.598	-1.061	-0.540	-0.824
D	-0.00001	-0.858	-0.00002	-2.024*
C	-0.003	0.053	-0.008	-1.143
W	0.008	1.672*	0.012	2.988*
S.E.E.	0.055		0.042	
R^2	0.486		0.507	

*Statistically significant at the .10 level.

Table 4-5

Summary of Regressions for Various Years (with Political Stability Variable)

Creditworthiness as function of variable	1971		1972		1973		1974	
	Coefficient	t-statistics	Coefficient	t-statistics	Coefficient	t-statistics	Coefficient	t-statistics
Constant	-0.892	-0.313	-2.980	-1.234	-7.571	-1.230	-7.302	-1.744*
GI	0.321	6.265*	0.266	7.649*	0.425	4.434*	0.312	3.749*
I	0.00003	1.522	0.00003	1.273	0.00001	0.147	-0.000001	-0.020
DSR	-0.874	-0.304	-2.988	-1.229	-7.600	-1.223	-7.320	-1.740*
RI	-0.070	-1.251	-0.044	-0.810	-0.048	-0.598	-0.701	-1.140
D	-0.00001	-0.702	-0.00001	-1.359	-0.0000	-0.153	-0.00001	-0.881
C	-0.0001	-1.020	0.0007	0.791	-0.0001	-0.195	0.0001	0.023
W	0.00009	1.434	-0.00001	-0.015	0.0007	0.204	0.0007	1.616
P	-0.00004	-0.866	-0.00001	-0.322	-0.0001	-1.139	0.00002	0.461
S.E.E.	0.0374		0.044		0.073		0.056	
R^2	0.677		0.757		0.501		0.491	

*Statistically significant at the .10 level

Table 4-6

Summary of Regressions Using Different Creditworthiness Indices
(for the Period 1971-1974 with Political Stability Variable)

Creditworthiness as function of variable	loan/GDP		loan/population		loan/need	
	Coefficient	t-statistics	Coefficient	t-statistics	Coefficient	t-statistics
Constant	-1.840	-2.174*	-750.53	-1.843*	-3.368	-1.962*
GI	0.004	0.312	-0.252	-0.377	0.297	10.535*
I	0.0000	0.750	0.021	7.969*	0.00002	1.498
DSR	-1.878	-2.203*	-763.000	-1.861*	-3.375	-1.953*
RI	-0.019	-1.284	3.155	0.443	-0.387	-1.289
D	-0.00001	-2.566*	-0.0025	-1.912*	-0.00001	-1.828*
C	-0.00001	-0.040	-0.119	-0.675	-0.0002	-0.284
W	0.00002	0.414	0.005	0.246	0.00007	0.934
P	-0.00001	-1.060	-0.018	-3.013*	-0.00002	-0.871
S.E.E.	0.025		12.318		0.052	
R^2	0.110		0.441		0.528	

*Statistically significant at the .10 level.

Table 4-7

Summary of Regressions Using Different Creditworthiness Indices
(for the Period 1971-1975)

Creditworthiness as function of variable	loan/GDP		loan/population		loan/need	
	Coefficient	t-statistics	Coefficient	t-statistics	Coefficient	t-statistics
Constant	-1.436	-2.158*	-382.37	-0.960	-2.861	-2.064*
GI	-0.020	-0.163	-7.626	-1.029	0.287	10.284*
I	0.0001	1.138	0.023	8.305*	0.00001	1.299
DSR	-1.467	-2.193*	-387.84	-0.968	-2.867	-2.056*
RI	-0.016	-1.240	1.410	0.181	-0.309	-1.143
D	-0.0001	-3.103*	-0.033	-2.240*	-0.0001	-2.350*
C	-0.001	-0.376	-0.003	-0.211	-0.0004	-0.811
W	0.0002	0.518	0.0064	0.023	0.00007	0.928
S.E.	0.024		14.862		0.052	
R^2	0.103		0.379		0.471	

*Statistically significant at the .10 level.

NOTES

[1]The sample was comprised of Argentina, Brazil, Chile, Republic of China (Taiwan), Colombia, Costa Rica, Dominican Republic, Egypt, El Salvador, Greece, Guatemala, Guyana, Honduras, India, Ivory Coast, Jamaica, Kenya, Korea, Malawi, Malaysia, Mexico, Morocco, Pakistan, Paraguay, Peru, Philippines, Sierra Leone, Sri Lanka, Sudan, Thailand, Turkey, Uruguay, and Zaire. The countries which had not borrowed at all from the private financial markets were excluded from the sample.

[2]Refer to the survey of Association of Reserve City Bankers in March 1977 mentioned on page 14 of this dissertation.

[3]The result of the estimation without the reserve/import ratio variable was as follows:

$$CW = \begin{array}{c} -2.666 \\ (-1.936) \end{array} + \begin{array}{c} 0.261 \ GI \\ (10.244)^* \end{array} + \begin{array}{c} 0.00001 \ I \\ (1.222) \end{array} - \begin{array}{c} 2.665 \ DSR \\ (-1.925)^* \end{array} - \begin{array}{c} 0.00001 \ D \\ (-2.377)^* \end{array}$$

$$\begin{array}{c} -0.0004 \ C \\ (-0.767) \end{array} + \begin{array}{c} 0.00008 \ W \\ (1.021) \end{array} \qquad\qquad (10)$$

$$R^2 = 0.466 \qquad S.E.E. = 0.052$$

*Statistically significant at the .05 level

[4]The function, including the ratio of the government revenue to GDP, was tested with the following results:

$$CW = \begin{array}{c} -2.529 \\ (-1.828) \end{array} + \begin{array}{c} 0.270 \ GI \\ (10.471)^* \end{array} + \begin{array}{c} 0.00002 \ I \\ (1.846)^{**} \end{array} - \begin{array}{c} 2.547 \ DSR \\ (-1.832)^{**} \end{array} - \begin{array}{c} 0.267 \ RI \\ (-0.992) \end{array}$$

$$\begin{array}{c} -0.00001 \ D \\ (-1.933)^{**} \end{array} - \begin{array}{c} 0.00055 \ C \\ (-1.018) \end{array} + \begin{array}{c} 0.00006 \ W \\ (0.819) \end{array} - \begin{array}{c} 0.0027G \\ (-1.986)^{**} \end{array} \qquad (11)$$

$$R^2 = 0.484 \qquad S.E.E. = 0.051$$

*Statistically significant at the .05 level

**Statistically significant at the .10 level

[5]Feierabend and Feierabend (1966) tested a sample of 84 nations for the seven-year period 1955-1961. The test results showed that "the distribution is skewed. Instability is more prevalent than stability within the sample of nations, and the largest proportion of countries are those experiencing an instability event with a scale weighting of 4."

[6]The estimation without the reserves/imports ratio was as follows:

$$CW = \begin{array}{cccccc} -3.179 & + & 0.292 \ GI & + & 0.00002 \ I & - & 3.181 \ DSR & - & 0.00001 \ D \\ (-1.854) & & (10.430)^* & & (1.370) & & (-1.843)^{**} & & (-1.799)^{**} \end{array}$$

$$\begin{array}{ccccc} -0.00027 \ C & + & 0.00008 \ W & - & 0.000028 \ P \\ (-0.368) & & (1.047) & & (-1.135) \end{array} \qquad (13)$$

$$R^2 = 0.521 \qquad S.E.E. = 0.052$$

**Significant at the .05 level

[7]The estimation without political stability variable for the period 1971-1974 yielded the following results:

$$CW = \begin{array}{cccccc} -2.846 & + & 0.295 \ GI & + & 0.00002 \ I & - & 2.843 \ DSR & - & 0.437 \ RI \\ (-1.772) & & (10.509)^* & & (1.505) & & (-1.761) & & (-1.484) \end{array}$$

$$\begin{array}{ccccc} -0.00001 \ D & - & 0.00006 \ C & + & 0.00007 \ W \\ (-1.995)^* & & (-0.091) & & (0.940) \end{array} \qquad (14)$$

$$R^2 = 0.525 \qquad S.E.E. = 0.052$$

[8]Some methods suggested to correct serial correlations are: (a) correlation of first differential, (b) correlation of cycles, (c) correlation of per capita data, (d) time as separate independent variables. See Dick A. Leabo, *Business Statistics* (Homewood, Ill.: Irwin, 1972), p. 445-50.

[9]This method has been suggested by Professor Roger Wright. The underlining idea of dividing the variables by their geometric means was to compare S.E.E. after eliminating the influence of heteroscedasticity. To do this, the original index (x_i) was tranformed to a new value $(Z_i) = x_i / GM(x)$, where $GM(x) = [\prod_{i=1}^{N} x_i]^{1/N}$.

CHAPTER V

CONCLUSIONS

The primary purpose of this study was to identify empirically the determinants of a country's creditworthiness, using a normative conceptual framework for creditworthiness. The study was motivated by the recent concern among the academic and professional communities about issues such as the optimum amount of foreign borrowing and how to assess the creditworthiness of LDCs. This concern has arisen because of (1) the change in the transfer mechanism of international capital flows from official sources to private commercial banks, in combination with a seemingly ever-increasing volume of borrowing by LDCs, and (2) widespread reports about the economic problems and debt reschedulings of several LDCs which had been major borrowers from private commercial markets.

The study begins with the premise that each bank has its own criteria for assessing risk and the debt repayment capability of a country. At present, most of the evaluations are based on the qualitative analysis or an index system using a number of common indicators, such as the debt-service ratio and the level of reserve to imports. The mechanics of constructing a country risk index vary widely from bank to bank. The indicators and their weights are subjectively determined by banks, in part based on their historical experience. The index system is a more objective criterion than the qualitative analysis in differentiating the creditworthiness among the countries. But because of subjective judgments in determining the indicators and their weights, the index score derived by this method is inevitably subjective.

There are few publicized attempts to devise a reliable statistical method of identifying creditworthiness. One reason for the lack of reliable statistical work in this area is that some key elements in assessing creditworthiness, i.e., political stability, willingness to pay, and the quality of external debt management, can hardly be quantified to fit into a statistical model. Thus, bankers rely on an eclectic approach, based on travel, working in an economy, and qualitative analyses which comprise the composite index technique of credit rating referred to above.

A more important reason for the insufficiency of any statistical studies on this issue is that no single creditor has experienced any *outright default* of repayment by a borrowing country since the 1930s. The lack of default experience makes it impossible to develop a model based on objective historical data. The dependent variable (creditworthiness) in the statistical model developed here cannot be obtained even on an *ex post* basis. Empirical tests based on actual incidents of rescheduling solve the problem of objectivity. But they do not answer the questions about outright default, or creditworthiness, which is an *ex ante* concept. This is because the approach based on rescheduling deals at best with the liquidity problem of a country.[1] Liquidity represents only one element of creditworthiness. It is not necessarily indicative of creditworthiness *per se*, which is a more comprehensive concept.

In this study an objective dependent variable, the creditworthiness index, was developed based on the actual volume of funds lent to LDCs from the private capital markets. Loan amounts were used as a proxy dependent variable, because the commercial banks lending to LDCs differentiate countries on the basis of country exposure limits. This procedure permits commercial banks to distribute their present and future risk assets on a country-by-country basis. Previous studies showed that credit rationing by the commercial banks is consistent with rational economic behavior of profit maximization in the presence of uncertainty. This behavior of banks is also documented by two 1977 surveys of the Association of Reserve City Bankers, and Export-Import Bank of the United States, which revealed that all the banks surveyed utilized formalized country exposure reporting procedures to set lending limits.

Based on this assumption or rationing by the commercial banks, the loan amounts supplied by the commercial banks were divided by the demand for such loans, that is, a country's need for external financing, so that the dependent variable, loan amounts divided by needs, ultimately became the creditworthiness index of a country with a value ranging between one and zero. The external financing needs were calculated by the Harrod-Domar model, which assessed capital requirements on an assumed common target growth rate, the respective savings ratio, and the applicable incremental capital-output ratio.

The conceptual framework for the creditworthiness (the explanatory variables for the model) was based on the economic analysis of foreign borrowings and derived from evaluation methods of the analysis of a firm's and/or a municipal unit's creditworthiness. All economic analyses for foreign borrowing, such as "foreign borrowing with instability of national income," "foreign borrowing with export revenue uncertainty," and "cumulative lending hypothesis," support the notion that optimal borrowing condition is at the point where the marginal product of capital equals the marginal interest cost of foreign borrowings. The productive use of foreign borrowing is reflected in the growth in national income. But the theoretical optimal borrowing condition for the borrower is not necessarily a sufficient condition for lenders, since the historical and anticipated profits or growth (optimal use of foreign capital) do not guarantee uninterrupted debt servicing or freedom from cash flow bottlenecks and unpredictable, temporary fluctuations in earnings. Cash flow and earnings fluctuations cannot be determined without evaluating a country's liquidity, debt structure, and coverage ratios, in addition to its profitability. In international lending, the sovereignty risk must also be considered. Commercial bankers emphasize the importance of a country's sovereignty risk, because even when the individual projects are economically feasible enough to permit borrowers to repay their obligations, the government of the country could prevent the borrower from complying with its obligations. Unlike domestic creditors, foreign lenders have, in effect, no recourse when a country is not willing to fulfill its obligations.

Starting from this basic framework, it was hypothesized that the creditworthiness of a country is a function of (1) growth in income (growth in GDP, growth in exports), (2) level of development (per capita income), (3) liquidity (change in debt service ratio, reserves/imports ratio), (4) debt structure (total outstanding debt/exports), (5) coverage ratio (debt service payment/net capital inflow), (6) willingness to pay (trends in the level of external financing to investment), and (7) political stability (political instability index).

Multiple regression analysis on the yearly data of the 33 LDCs from 1971 to 1975 supported the hypotheses established in this study. The stability of the model was confirmed through three different exercises: (1) a test of stability of the creditworthiness index, (2) a test on the temporal observations using yearly data, and (3) a test using average values of yearly data.

The signs of all coefficients except the reserves/imports ratio were as expected. Among these explanatory variables, growth in GDP, expected change in the debt service ratio, and the debt/exports ratio were important variables.   The growth in GDP was the most important variable and was absolutely significant at all levels.

The importance of this finding is its reconfirmation that, from a long-run point of view, foreign borrowing is justified only to the extent that the marginal product of capital is greater than the marginal interest cost of foreign borrowings. For consistent growth in GDP to materialize, public and private consumption should not be allowed to rise at a rate that exceeds the growth in GDP and "the savings out of newly generated income must be sufficient to enable the economy to finance an increasing proportion of its own investment requirements out of domestic resources."[2]   In previous studies based on the reschedulings, growth in GDP was not considered an important determinant of the creditworthiness of a country, because these studies dealt only with the liquidity problem of rescheduled countries, but not with the "profit-ability" issue.

The empirical results on the liquidity ratios indicated that the absolute level of the debt service ratio at any point in time was important largely in relation to possible future change in that ratio. Contrary to the generally held belief, the debt-service ratio in the year (t-1) was positively related to the creditworthiness index, and the reserves/imports ratio was negatively related. But the coefficient for the change in expected debt service was negatively related to the creditworthiness index, as hypothesized.

The result regarding the debt service ratio can be explained by the fact that, in the initial stage of external borrowings, bankers might recognize that the debt service ratio will, inevitably, increase quickly with a relatively higher amount of external borrowings, and will attain a high level. As a result of temporary bottlenecks in reallocating resources to exports or import substitution due to rigidities in the internal economic structure, or external obstacles that cut export growth, many countries with a higher debt-service ratio might still be regarded as creditworthy as long as they could invest the borrowed funds in productive assets and repay without serious debt servicing difficulties. Since economic growth is continuous, the structural change of the economy will inevitably remove any temporary bottleneck to the reallocation of resources, with a consequent rise in exports.

The empirical result on the debt structure as a determinant of creditworthiness reconfirmed that the high ratio of debt of GDP is not always a serious indication of lack of creditworthiness without considering the use of the funds borrowed externally. The coefficient of the debt/GDP was not statistically significant. For the analysis of debt structure as an indicator of long-term liquidity, debt/exports was a more relevant indicator. It was negatively related to creditworthiness and was significant at the .05 level. Bankers might better consider the balance between the level of debt and the exports rather than the value between the level of debt and GDP.

The coverage ratio, willingness to pay, and political stability indicators all were related to the creditworthiness index as expected, but they were not statistically significant.

Limitations and Contributions of the Study

This study has developed creditworthiness indices of LDCs based on the actual loan amounts from the private capital markets and has proceeded to analyze the determinants of creditworthiness within a normative conceptual framework. However, the application of this study to the general explanation of a country's creditworthiness is partially limited by two assumptions made in the study: (1) the target income growth rate used for the creditworthiness index is constant to all countries and time periods. (2) Commercial banks ration their loans to LDCs based on past patterns of economic and political behavior.

The first assumption was based on the argument that every LDC wants economic development as rapidly as possible, and that rapid development is constrained by whether the country can find an investment project which yields more than the cost of borrowing. In this sense, the target growth rate will be infinite within the constraints of the absorptive capacity of the country and the availability of the investment projects. The actual target growth rates of all LDCs have already reflected those constraints, and those cannot be the unconstrained (desired) target growth rates. Thus, to compare objectively the creditworthiness of countries, the limitation on the absorptive capacity and the availability of investment projects to each country should not be considered. Under these circumstances, the same target for income growth should be applied equally to every country. One question to be answered in this assumption is which particular target rate should be applied.

A counter-argument for this assumption would be that there are different desired target rates for different countries. Even though the absorptive capacity and the availability of the investment projects are unlimited, countries may not try to develop as fast as possible. Most countries try to harmonize their rapid economic development with their economic and political stability. A practical problem of this argument is that there is no way to determine the unconstrained desired target growth rate for each country.

On the issue of which one particular target growth rate should be applied, the first assumption was justified in this study by a test of stability of the creditworthiness index values based on different target growth rates. The test shows that the result of any one regression using a certain target growth rate was not substantially different from those of other regressions using different target growth rates.

The second assumption in this study was that the rationing of loans to LDCs by the commercial banks is based on the past pattern of economic and political behavior. Many say that lending is an art and not a science. Bankers have to take into account not only what was the growth in GDP, but also what it is likely to be in the future. First-hand experience and qualitative analysis are included in the evaluation; bankers will evaluate the competence of the present administrators of the country and may visualize how the country will react on debt service difficulties, if any. These arguments are reasonable and acceptable, but this shortcoming of the second assumption can exist in any econometric model based on the *ex post* data.

Notwithstanding the limitations arising from the two assumptions, this study has answered many important questions about evaluating the creditworthiness of countries. It has developed for the first time an objective creditworthiness index, it has provided a conceptual framework within which relevant data and forecast can be conveniently analyzed, and it has assigned weights (or importance) to the relevant indicators of creditworthiness using statistical methods rather than subjective judgments.

Hopefully, this study will facilitate the understanding of the subjective evaluation of the creditworthiness of a country and will provide public and private policymakers with parameters within which to formulate better external borrowing or lending strategies.

NOTES

[1]One may even argue that some reschedulings have been motivated by a country's desire to obtain better terms on previously contracted debt.

[2]D. Avaramovic, et al., op. cit., p. 88.

APPENDIX I

Reschedulings Included in the Three Major Studies Based on Rescheduling
(Period 1959-1972)

Rescheduled Country	Years when payments deferred	Frank & Cline (1960-68)	Dhonte (1959-71)	Feder & Just (1965-72)
Argentina	1961-62	1961	1962	--
	1963-64	1963	--	--
	1965	1965	--	1965
Brazil	1961	1961	1961	--
	1963**	--	--	--
	1964	1964	--	--
Chile	1965-66	1965	1965	1965
	1972	N/A	N/A	1972
Costa Rica	1962**	--	--	--
	1965**	--	--	--
Egypt	1966-67*	1967	1966	1966
Ghana	1966-68	1966	1965	1966
	1969-70	--	--	1969
				1970
	1972	N/A	N/A	1972
India	1968	1968	--	1968
	1969	N/A	--	1969
	1972	N/A	N/A	--
Indonesia	1966-67	1966	--	1966
	1968	1968	1968	--
	1969	N/A	--	1970
	1971	N/A	--	--
Liberia	1963*	--	--	--
	1969**	--	--	--
Mali	1966**	--	--	--
Pakistan	1971	N/A	--	1971
Peru	1968	--	1968	1968
	1969	N/A	N/A	1969
Philippines	1970*	--	1970	--

Rescheduled Country	Years when payments deferred	Frank & Cline (1960-68)	Dhonte (1959-71)	Feder & Just (1965-72)
Turkey	1958	N/A	1959	N/A
	1965	1965	1965	1965
	1968	1968	--	1968
	1972c	N/A	--	1970
Uruguay	1965*	--	1965	1965
				1968
Yugoslavia	1965*	--	1965	1966
	1971*	N/A	1971	--
		13 cases	13 cases	21 cases

*   : Bilateral reschedulings
** : U.S. Export-Import Bank reschedulings
c   : Dates of agreements to reschedule arrears
N/A: Not applicable

Source: (1) C. Frank and W. Cline, "Measurement of Debt Serving Capacity: An Application of Discriminant Analysis," *Journal of International Economics*, No. 1, 1971, p. 328.

(2) P. Dhonte, "Describing External Debt Situations: A Rollover Approach," *International Monetary Fund Staff Papers*, March 1975, p. 183.

(3) G. Feder and R. Just, "A Study of Debt Servicing Capacity Applying Logit Analysis," *Journal of Development Economics*, March 1977, p. 31.

(4) H. Bittermann, *The Refunding of International Debt*, p. 84.

APPENDIX II

Definition of Irregular Political Events*

(1) *Dismissals or resignations of officeholders:* Major cabinet changes or executive power changes; (a) Major cabinet changes, defined as the number of times in a year that a new premier is named and/or 50 percent of the cabinet posts are occupied by new ministers; (b) The number of times in a year that effective control of the executive power changes hands. Such change requires that the new executive be independent of his predecessor.

(2) *Strikes:* Any strike of 1,000 or more industrial or service workers that involves more than one employer and that is aimed at national government policies or authority.

(3) *Demonstrations:* Any peaceful public gathering of at least 100 people for the primary purpose of displaying or voicing their opposition to government policies or authority, excluding demonstrations of a distinctly anti-foreign nature.

(4) *Riots:* Any violent demonstration or clash of more than 100 citizens involving the use of physical force.

(5) *Assassinations:* Any politically motivated murder or attempted murder of a high government official or politician.

(6) *Arrests and imprisonments:* Any systematic elimination by jailing or execution of political opposition within the ranks of the regime or the opposition.

(7) *Revolts:* Any illegal or forced change in the top governmental elite, any attempt at such a change, or any successful or unsuccessful armed rebellion whose aim is independence from the central government.

(8) *Coups d'etat:* The number of extraconstitutional or forced changes in the top government elite and/or its effective control of the nation's power structure in a given year. The term "coup" includes, but is not exhausted by, the term "successful revolution." Unsuccessful coups are not counted.

(9) *Guerrilla:* Any armed activity, sabotage, or bombings carried on by independent bands of citizens or irregular forces and aimed at the overthrow of the present regime.

*The description of each irregular event used for the political stability index is paraphrased from "Cross-National Time Series: 1815-1973," 1976, by the Inter-university Consortium for Political and Social Research (ICPSR), Ann Arbor, Michigan.

APPENDIX III

Stepwise (Forward) Regression on the Creditworthiness Index

SELECTION OF REGRESSION   O=STEPWISE,FORWARD L=.2,.2

ANALYSIS AT STEP 1 FOR 151.HARROD 4   N= 165 OUT OF 165

SOURCE	DF	SUM OF SQRS	MEAN SQUARE	F-STAT	SIGNIF
REGRESSION	1	.33404	.33404	118.37	.0000
ERROR	163	.45997	.28219 -2		
TOTAL	164	.79401			

MULTIPLE R= .64861   R-SQR= .42070   SE= .53122 -1

VARIABLE	PARTIAL	COEFFICIENT	STD ERROR	T-STAT	SIGNIF
CONSTANT		-.16283 -1	.76489 -2	-2.1288	.0348
234.GROWTH I	.64861	.27762	.25516 -1	10.880	.0000

REMAINING	PARTIAL	SIGNIF
203.RESV IM	-.06327	.4209
276.DSR	-.13575	.0831
269.WILLING	.07289	.3536
401.DEBT EX	-.16572	.0340
402.INCOME	.16154	.0388
213.COVERAGE	-.05435	.4894
271.GOVERNT	-.14200	.0697

ANALYSIS AT STEP 2 FOR 151.HARROD 4   N= 165 OUT OF 165

SOURCE	DF	SUM OF SQRS	MEAN SQUARE	F-STAT	SIGNIF
REGRESSION	2	.34667	.17334	62.772	.0000
ERROR	162	.44734	.27614 -2		
TOTAL	164	.79401			

MULTIPLE R= .66076   R-SQR= .43661   SE= .52549 -1

VARIABLE	PARTIAL	COEFFICIENT	STD ERROR	T-STAT	SIGNIF
CONSTANT		-.34616 -2	.96533 -2	-.35859	.7204
234.GROWTH I	.63447	.26793	.25645 -1	10.448	.0000
401.DEBT EX	-.16572	-.10366 -4	.48464 -5	-2.1388	.0340

REMAINING	PARTIAL	SIGNIF
203.RESV IM	-.05543	.4822
276.DSR	-.18648	.0171
269.WILLING	.07179	.3624
402.INCOME	.14032	.0740
213.COVERAGE	-.06316	.4232
271.GOVERNT	-.12288	.1181

ANALYSIS AT STEP 3 FOR 151.HARROD 4 N= 165 OUT OF 165

SOURCE	DF	SUM OF SQRS	MEAN SQUARE	F-STAT	SIGNIF
REGRESSION	3	.36223	.12074	45.022	.0000
ERROR	161	.43179	.26819 -2		
TOTAL	164	.79401			

MULTIPLE R= .67543 R-SQR= .45620 SE= .51787 -1

VARIABLE	PARTIAL	COEFFICIENT	STD ERROR	T-STAT	SIGNIF
CONSTANT		-3.1657	1.3130	-2.4111	.0170
276.DSR	-.18648	-3.1751	1.3183	-2.4085	.0171
234.GROWTH I	.62621	.25983	.25495 -1	10.191	.0000
401.DEBT EX	-.20895	-.13389 -4	.49383 -5	-2.7111	.0074

REMAINING	PARTIAL	SIGNIF
203.RESV IM	-.08625	.2751
269.WILLING	.07147	.3661
402.INCOME	.08980	.2558
213.COVERAGE	-.06713	.3960
271.GOVERNT	-.12278	.1196

```
ANALYSIS AT STEP 4 FOR 151.HARROD 4   N= 165 OUT OF 165

SOURCE            DF    SUM OF SQRS   MEAN SQUARE   F-STAT    SIGNIF

REGRESSION         4      .36874      .92185  -1    34.682    .0000
ERROR            160      .42528      .26580  -2
TOTAL            164      .79401

MULTIPLE R= .68147   R-SQR= .46440   SE= .51556  -1


VARIABLE       PARTIAL   COEFFICIENT   STD ERROR    T-STAT    SIGNIF

CONSTANT                  -3.1277      1.3074      -2.3924    .0179
276.DSR        -.18642    -3.1501      1.3125      -2.4001    .0175
234.GROWTH I    .63162     .26192      .25416  -1   10.305    .0000
401.DEBT EX    -.19354    -.12374  -4  .49588  -5   -2.4953   .0136
271.GOVERNT    -.12278    -.20405  -2  .13039  -2   -1.5649   .1196


REMAINING      PARTIAL   SIGNIF

203.RESV IM    -.07395    .3512
269.WILLING     .06057    .4453
402.INCOME      .13629    .0847
213.COVERAGE   -.08176    .3025
```

```
ANALYSIS AT STEP 5 FOR 151.HARROD 4  N= 165 OUT OF 165

SOURCE          DF    SUM OF SQRS   MEAN SQUARE   F-STAT    SIGNIF

REGRESSION       5      .37664       .75328 -1    28.696    .0000
ERROR          159      .41738       .26250 -2
TOTAL          164      .79401

MULTIPLE R= .68873    R-SQR= .47435    SE= .51235 -1

VARIABLE       PARTIAL   COEFFICIENT   STD ERROR    T-STAT    SIGNIF

CONSTANT                  -2.3744      1.3699      -1.7333    .0850
276.DSR        -.13629    -2.3877      1.3764      -1.7348    .0847
234.GROWTH I    .63809     .26435       .25297 -1   10.450    .0000
401.DEBT EX    -.15168    -.99207 -5    .51269 -5   -1.9351    .0548
402.INCOME      .13629     .17090 -4    .98515 -5    1.7348    .0847
271.GOVERNT    -.15973    -.27850 -2    .13650 -2   -2.0403    .0430

REMAINING      PARTIAL    SIGNIF

203.RESV IM    -.08147     .3058
269.WILLING     .07462     .3484
213.COVERAGE   -.08176     .3040
```

REGRESSION OF 151.HARROD 4 USING FORWARD SELECTION

STEP	R-SQR	STD ERROR	# VAR	VARIABLE		PARTIAL	SIGNIF
1	.42070	.53122 -1	1	234.GROWTH I	IN	.64861	.0000
2	.43661	.52549 -1	2	401.DEBT EX	IN	-.16572	.0340
3	.45620	.51787 -1	3	276.DSR	IN	-.18648	.0171
4	.46440	.51556 -1	4	271.GOVERNT	IN	-.12278	.1196
5	.47435	.51235 -1	5	402.INCOME	IN	.13629	.0847

APPENDIX IV

Average Creditworthiness Indices of Sample Countries
(for the Period 1971-1975)

Country	Index (Y)	Fitted Value*(Y)
Taiwan	.196	.123
Brazil	.176	.186
Peru	.145	.074
Dominican Rep.	.121	.102
Malaysia	.120	.083
Korea	.106	.111
Ivory Coast	.100	.065
Mexico	.081	.060
Costa Rica	.080	.067
Zaire	.072	.101
Greece	.062	.082
Philippines	.059	.055
Morocco	.058	.035
El Salvador	.055	.044
Paraguay	.043	.041
Argentina	.042	.042
Uruguay	.040	.008
Egypt	.036	.052
Jamaica	.033	.082
Colombia	.032	.049
Sudan	.031	.039
Guyana	.022	.011
Guatemala	.021	.031
Turkey	.006	.058
Pakistan	.006	-.003
Thailand	.005	.074
Sierra Leone	.005	.039
Kenya	.005	.039
Malawi	.005	.022
Chile	.005	.002
Honduras	.003	-.003
India	.003	-.004
Sri Lanka	.001	-.012

*The figures are fitted values from equation (13) in Chapter IV.

BIBLIOGRAPHY

Agtmael, Antoine W. van, "Evaluating the Risks of Lending to Developing Countries," *Euromoney*, April 1976, pp. 16-30.

Ake, Claude, "A Definition of Political Stability," *Comparative Politics*, January 1975, pp. 271-283.

Alter, Gerald M., "The Servicing of Foreign Capital Inflows by Underdeveloped Countries," in H.S. Ellis, ed., *Economic Development of Latin America*, New York: St. Martin's Press, pp. 139-167.

Asian Finance, "Technique of Credit Rationing: BOA Methodology," 15 September/14 October 1977, pp. 46-47.

Association of Reserve City Bankers, *Country Exposure Measurement and Reporting Practices of Member Bankers*, March 1977.

Avaramovic, Dragoslav, et al., *Economic Growth and External Debt*, Baltimore, Md.: The Johns Hopkins Press, 1964.

Avaramovic, Dragoslav and Gulhati, Ravi I., *Debt Servicing Problems of Low-income Countries, 1956-1958*, Baltimore, Md.: The Johns Hopkins Press, 1960.

Azzi, Carry F. and Cox, James C., "A Theory and Test of Credit Rationing: Comment," *The American Economic Review*, December 1976, pp. 911-915.

Bade, Robin, "Optimal Growth and Foreign Borrowing with Restricted Mobility of Foreign Capital," *International Economic Review*, October 1972, pp. 544-552.

Bank for International Settlements, *Annual Report*, various issues.

Bank of England, *Quarterly Bulletin*, various issues.

Bee, Robert N., "Lessons from Debt Reschedulings in the Past," *Euromoney*, April 1977, pp. 33-36.

Bee, Robert N., "Syndication," in F.J. Mathis, ed., *Offshore Lending by U.S. Commercial Banks*, Washington, D.C.: Bankers' Association for Foreign Trade and Robert Morris Associates.

Beek, David C., "Commercial Bank Lending to the Developing Countries," *Quarterly Review*, Federal Reserve Bank of New York, Summer 1977, pp. 1-8.

Bittermann, Henry J., *The Refunding of International Debt*, Durham, N.C.: Duke University Press, 1973.

Brackenridge, A. Bruce, "Evaluating Country Credits," *Institutional Investors,* June 1977, pp. 13-16.

Brackenridge, A. Bruce, "Techniques of Credit Rating," *Asian Finance,* 15 September/14 October 1977, pp. 46-53.

Brimmer, Andrew F., "International Capital Markets and the Financing of Economic Development," Paper presented at the inaugural lecture in the Samuel Z. Westerfield, Jr., Distinguished Lecture Series, Atlanta University, 1973.

Chase Manhattan Bank, *Euro-Dollar Financing,* New York, April 1968.

Cheng, Hang-Sheng, *International Bond Issues of the Less-Developed Countries,* Ames, Iowa: The Iowa State University Press, 1969.

Cleveland, Harold von Baron and Brittain, W.H. Bruce, "Developing Countries' External Debt and the Private Banks," (mimeographed), March 1977.

Cleveland, Harold von Baron and Brittain, W.H. Bruce, "Are the LDCs in Over Their Heads?," *The Foreign Affairs,* July 1977, pp. 732-750.

Costanzo, G.A., "Lending to Developing Countries--Why The Gloom is Overdone," *The Banker,* June 1976, pp. 581-583.

Costanzo, G.A., "Is the Third World a Sound Debtor?," *New York Times,* April 8, 1976.

Davis, Steven I., *The Euro-Bank: Its Origins, Management and Outlook,* New York: John Wiley & Sons, 1976.

Davis, Steven I., "How Risky is International Lending?," *Harvard Business Review,* Jan.-Feb. 1977, pp. 135-143.

Dhonte, Pierre, "Describing External Debt Situations: A Roll-over Approach," *IMF Staff Papers,* March 1975, pp. 159-186.

Diaz-Alejandro, Carlos, "Less Developed Countries and the Post-1971 International Financial System," *Essays in International Finance,* No. 108, Princeton University, April 1975.

Dufey, Gunter and Giddy, Ian H., *The International Money Market,* Englewood Cliffs, N.J.: Printice-Hall, 1978.

Dufey, Gunter and Giddy, Ian H., "The Determination of Eurocurrency Interest Rates," Working Paper No. 108, Ann Arbor, Mich.: Graduate School of Business Administration, The University of Michigan, February 1976.

Dufey, Gunter and Min, Sangkee, "The Access of Developing Countries to International Credit," Working Paper No. 148, Ann Arbor, Mich.: Graduate School of Business Administration, The University of Michigan, July 1977.

Duff, Declan and Peacock, Ian, "A Cash-flow Approach to Sovereign Risk Analysis," *The Banker*, January 1977, pp. 55-61.

Einzig, Paul and Quinn, Brian Scott, *The Euro-Dollar System: Practices and Theory of International Interest Rates*, London: The Macmillan Press, 1977.

Export-Import Bank of the United States, "A Survey of Country Evaluation Systems in Use," (mimeographed), December 22, 1976.
Feder, Gershon and Just, Richard E., "A Study of Debt Servicing Capacity Applying

Logit Analysis," *Journal of Development Economics*, March 1977, pp. 25-38.

The Federal Reserve Board, et al., "Country Exposure Survey," January 16, 1978.

Feierabend, Ivo K., et al., "The Comparative Study of Revolution and Violence," *Comparative Politics*, April 1973, pp. 393-424.

Frank, Charles R., Jr. and Cline, William R., "Measurement of Debt Servicing Capacity: An Application of Discriminant Analysis," *Journal of International Economics*, No. 1, 1971, pp. 327-344.

Freimer, Marshall and Gordon, Myron J., "Why Bankers Ration Credit," *Quarterly Journal of Economics*, April 1965, pp. 397-416.

Friedman, Benjamin M., "Credit Rationing: A Review," *Staff Economic Studies*, No. 72, Board of Governors of the Federal Reserve System, 1972.

Friedman, Irving S., *The Emerging Role of Private Banks in the Developing World*, New York: Citicorp, 1977.

Friedman, Irving S., "Country Risk: The Lessons of Zaire," *The Banker*, February 1978, pp. 29-31.

Friscia, A. Blake, "Creditworthiness of a Country," *The Bankers Magazine*, December 1973, pp. 31-36.

Giddy, Ian H. and Ray, Russ, "The Eurodollar Market and the Third World," *Business Review*, The University of Michigan, March 1976, pp. 11-15.

Goodman, Stephen, "How the Big U.S. Banks Really Evaluate Sovereign Risk," *Euromoney*, February 1977, pp. 105-110.

Green, Robert T. and Korth, Christopher M., "Political Instability and the Foreign Investor," *California Management Review*, Fall 1974, pp. 23-31.

Hagen, Everett E., *The Economics of Development*, Homewood, Ill.: Richard D. Irwin, 1975.

Hawkins, E.K., "Measuring Capital Requirements," *Development and Finance*, June 1968, pp. 2-7.

Hawkins, Robert G., Ness, Ealter L., Jr., and Sakong, H., "Improving the Access of Developing Countries to the U.S. Capital Market," *The Bulletin*, Graduate School of Business Administration, New York University, 1975.

Hayes, Douglas A., *Bank Lending Policies: Domestic and International*, Michigan Business Studies, New Series, Vol. 1, No. 3, Ann Arbor, Mich.: Bureau of Business Research, The University of Michigan, 1977.

Henning, Charles N., Pigott, William and Scott, Robert Haney, *International Financial Management*, New York: McGraw-Hill, 1978.

Hibbs, Douglas A., Jr., *Mass Political Violence: A Cross-National Causal Analysis*, New York: John Wiley & Sons, 1973.

International Monetary Fund, *Annual Report*, various issues.

International Monetary Fund, *International Financial Statistics*, various issues.

Jaffe, Dwight M., and Modigliani, Franco, "A Theory and Test of Credit Rationing," *American Economic Review*, December 1969, pp. 850-872.

Jaffe, Dwight M., and Modigliani, Franco, "A Theory and Test of Credit Rationing: Reply," *American Economic Review*, December 1976, pp. 919-920.

Kapur, Ishan, "An Analysis of the Supply of Euro-Currency Finance to Developing Countries," *Oxford Bulletin of Economics and Statistics*, August 1977, pp. 171-188.

Kindleberger, Charles P., *Economic Development*, New York: McGraw-Hill, 1965.

Kindleberger, Charles P., *International Economics* (5th edition), Homewood, Ill.: Richard D. Irwin, 1973.

Koldor, Nicholas, "A Model of Economic Growth," *Economic Journal*, December 1957, pp. 591-624.

Kuznets, Simon S., *Modern Economic Growth: Rate, Structure and Spread*, New Haven: Yale University Press, 1966.

Liddell, Andrew, "Syndicated Eurocredits: The Drift Towards the Big Banks," *The Banker*, November 1976, pp. 1221-1223.

Lissakers, Karin, *International Debt, the Banks, and U.S. Foreign Policy*, A Staff Report Prepared for the Use of Subcommittee on Foreign Economic Policy of the Committee on Foreign Relations, United States Senate, Washington, D.C.: U.S. Government Printing Office, August 1977.

Little, Jane Sneddon, "The Euro-dollar Market: Its Nature and Impact," *New England Economic Review*, Federal Reserve Bank of Boston, May-June 1969, pp. 2-31.

Little, Jane Sneddon, *Eurodollars: The Money Market Gypsies*, New York: Harper & Row, 1975.

Loser, Claudio M., "External Debt Management and Balance of Payments Policies," *IMF Staff Papers*, March 1977, pp. 168-192.

Maroni, Yves, "Approaches for Accessing the Risk Involved to Developing Countries," *International Finance Discussion Papers*, Number 112, Federal Reserve Board, November 1977.

McCabe, James L. and Sibley, David S., "Optimal Foreign Debt Accumulation with Export Revenue Uncertainty," *International Economic Review*, October 1976, pp. 675-685.

Michalopoulos, Constantine, "Payments Arrangements for Less Developed Countries: The Role of Foreign Assistance," *Essays in International Finance*, No. 102, Princeton University, November 1973.

Michalopoulos, Constantine, "Financing Needs of Developing Countries: Proposals for International Action," *Essays in International Finance*, No. 110, Princeton University, June 1975.

Mikesell, Raymond F., *U.S. Private and Government Investment Abroad*, Eugene, Ore.: University of Oregon, 1962.

Mikesell, Raymond F., *Public International Lending for Development*, New York: Random House, 1966.

Mohammed, Azizali F. and Saccomanni, Fabrizio, "Short-Term Banking and Euro-Currency Credits to Developing Countries," *IMF Staff Papers*, November 1973, pp. 612-638.

Monson, Robert A., "Political Stability in Mexico: The Changing Role of Traditional Rights," *The Journal of Politics*, August 1973, pp. 594-614.

Nagy, P. "The Debt Service Ratio--How Useful a Tool?," *The Banker*, April 1976, pp. 347-350.

Porter, Richard C. and Hutcheson, Tomas L., "The Cost of Tying Aid: A Method and Some Colombian Estimates," *Essays in International Finance*, No. 30, Princeton University, March 1972.

Quinn, Brian Scott, *The New Euromarkets*, New York: John Wiley & Sons, 1975.

Rosenstein-Rodan, P., "International Aid for Underdeveloped Countries," *The Review of Economics and Statistics*, May 1961, pp. 107-138.

Ruckdesched, Fred B., "Risk in Foreign and Domestic Lending Activities of U.S. Banks," *International Finance Discussion Papers*, No. 66, Federal Reserve Board, 1975.

Sargen, Nicholas P., "Commercial Bank Lending to Developing Countries," *Economic Review*, Federal Reserve Bank of San Francisco, March 1976, pp. 20-31.

Solow, Robert, "A Contribution of the Theory of Economic Growth," *Quarterly Journal of Economics*, February 1956, pp. 65-94.

Tsurutani, Taketsugu, "Stability and Instability," *The Journal of Politics*, November 1968, pp. 910-933.

Twentieth Century Fund, Task Force on the Municipal Bond Market, *Building a Broader Market*, New York, McGraw-Hill, 1976.

United Nations: *Yearbook of International Trade Statistics*, various years.

UNCTAD, *Debt Problems of Developing Countries*, TD/B/545/Rev. 1, March 7, 1975.

UNCTAD, *Debt Problems in the Context of Development*, TD/B/C.3/109/Rev. 1, 1974.

UNCTAD, *Present Institutional Arrangement for Debt Renegotiation*, TD/B/C.3/AC. 8/13, February 12, 1975.

U.S. Treasury, *Outlook for International Lending by U.S. Banks*, August 1976.

Van Horne, James C., *Financial Management and Policy*, Englewood Cliffs, N.J.: Prentice-Hall, 1977.

Willett, Thomas D., "The Oil-Transfer Problem and International Economic Stability," *Essays in International Finance*, No. 113, Princeton University, December 1975.

The World Bank, *Borrowing in International Capital Markets*, various issues.

The World Bank, *World Debt Tables*, Volume I and II, 1977.

The World Bank, *World Tables 1976*, 1976.

The World Bank, *Multinational Debt Renegotiations Since 1956*, May 1973.

Wright, Roger L. and Spivey, W. Allen, "Exploratory Analysis of Multivariate Data for Business Research," Working Paper No. 130, Ann Arbor, Mich.: Graduate School of Business Administation, The University of Michigan, May 1976.

Wright, Roger L., "Introduction to MIDAS for Business Administration Applications," (mimeográphed) Graduate School of Business Administration, The University of Michigan, May 1978.

INDEX